Go Listen to the Crofters

Go Listen to the Crofters

A. D. Cameron

The Napier Commission and Crofting a Century Ago

The publisher acknowledges financial subsidy from The Scottish Arts
Council towards the publication of this volume.

The publishers are also grateful for financial assistance from the Highlands and
Islands Development Board.

For Elsbeth
© 1986 A. D. Cameron

First published in Scotland in 1986 by Acair Ltd, Unit 8a, 7 James St., Stornoway,
Isle of Lewis.

First reprint in Scotland in 1990 by Acair Ltd., Unit 8a, 7 James St., Stornoway,
Isle of Lewis.

Designed by Jim Thomson Graphic Design, Muir of Ord.
Printed by Nevisprint, Fort William.

ISBN 0 86152 063 7

Contents

The Napier Commission and Crofting a Century Ago

Author's Acknowledgements
I wish to record my gratitude for all the assistance given to me during the writing of this book by the staffs of the National Library of Scotland, the Scottish Record Office and the Scottish Room of Edinburgh City Library. For help in tracing interesting photographs of the period, I wish to thank the staffs of Aberdeen University Library and the Scottish Ethnological Archive of the National Museums of Scotland, and Robert N Smart of St Andrews University. It is a pleasure to thank Annie MacPherson of Lower Milovaig, grand-daughter of John MacPherson, and Alister Ross of Portree for help in Skye; John Campbell, Mary Kate MacKinnon and Mary Sarah MacNeil for help in Barra; and the drivers of the post buses for sharing their local knowledge in North Uist. Specially to be thanked are R W and Jean Munro who brought their knowledge of Highland history and skills in editing to reading the whole text, which helped to remove errors and develop new lines of enquiry.

Publisher's Acknowledgements
Documents illustrating the written information collected by the Napier Commission are reproduced by kind permission of the Controller of H.M. Stationery Office and the copyright photographs by kind permission of:

George Washington Wilson Collection, Aberdeen University Library, pages 38, 46, 47, 77

Acair Ltd, page 30

By courtesy of Edinburgh City Libraries, pages v, vi, 15, 20, 25, 28, 33, 45, 51, 55, 85, 91, 105, 106, 110

Gordon Harvey, page 76

R W Munro, page 62

The Trustee of the National Galleries of Scotland, Edinburgh, page 120

National Library of Scotland, pages Front Cover, Title page, vii, 4, 31, 34, 36, 40, 63, 78, 83, 90, 91, 102, 115, 125

Orkney Library, page 94

Royal Commission on Ancient Monuments Scotland, pages 59, 69, 97, 100, 107

St Andrews University, pages 26, 37, 50, 99

Scottish Ethnological Archive, National Museums of Scotland, pages 22, 29, 81, 82, 86, 88, 98, 109, 118

Shetland Library, pages 41, 88

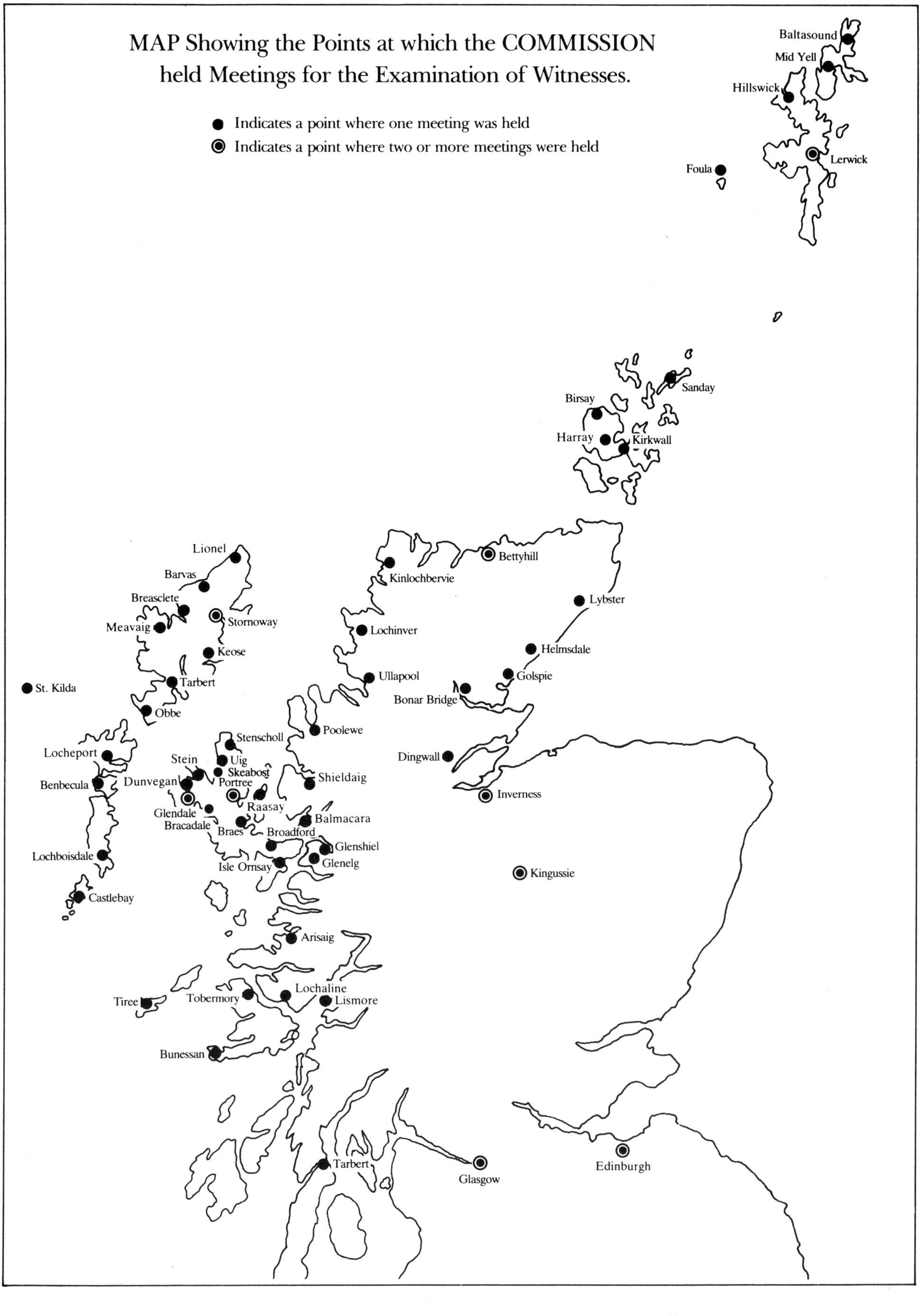

MAP Showing the Points at which the COMMISSION held Meetings for the Examination of Witnesses.

● Indicates a point where one meeting was held

◉ Indicates a point where two or more meetings were held

Baltasound

Mid Yell

Hillswick

Foula

Lerwick

Birsay

Sanday

Harray

Kirkwall

Bettyhill

Lionel

Barvas

Kinlochbervie

Lybster

Breasclete

Stornoway

Meavaig

Lochinver

Helmsdale

Keose

Golspie

Tarbert

Ullapool

St. Kilda

Bonar Bridge

Obbe

Poolewe

Dingwall

Locheport

Stenscholl

Stein

Uig

Benbecula

Dunvegan

Skeabost

Shieldaig

Inverness

Portree

Glendale

Raasay

Bracadale

Balmacara

Braes

Broadford

Lochboisdale

Isle Ornsay

Glenshiel

Glenelg

Kingussie

Castlebay

Arisaig

Tiree

Tobermory

Lochaline

Lismore

Bunessan

Tarbert

Glasgow

Edinburgh

Introduction

What was it like to be a crofter a hundred years ago? How far were the crofters able to provide for their basic needs from their land? Did they farm with hand tools like the spade and the *caschrom* (crooked spade or foot plough) by choice? Did they carry home peats in creels because that had always been their way? Did they build their own houses? Did the women spin the wool from their own sheep on the spinning wheel and did the men weave the cloth to make the family clothes? Did the women still go up to the *shielings* and stay there minding the cattle in summer? And did the people often hold informal gatherings called *ceilidhs*, where they would tell stories, play the bagpipes, and dance and sing?

Many of these are ingredients of the traditional view of earlier crofting life but our picture is often less reliable than it might be. Few people living on crofts thought of writing about it at the time, and frequently what we know is drawn from memory. When asked what life was like in their young days, many old people fortunately can reach back over the years and describe in amazing detail old ways of doing things or incidents which impressed themselves on their minds. But old people also forget sometimes. They may also embroider their stories in telling and re-telling them, or hone them sharp to give an edge to their conclusion. They know that everybody likes a good story, and a good story-teller. Things get worse when, years later, other people try to recount what older people have told them. Their accounts may be vivid but they may not always be true.

Skye crofter and his wife, she grinding grain with the quern outside the house he built.

Memories of the past can also become less than true in other ways. A task one man hated as a child simply through his own lack of skill may be remembered as difficult or distasteful, while another's childhood memories of caring parents, poor though they may have been, can transform his impression of his earlier years into a long-lost golden age. Descendants of crofting families now living very different lives in cities or in distant lands must have ideas about the old home and the way of life of their ancestors which are imperfect, and perhaps quite fanciful at times. With distance and the passage of time, nostalgia sets in as they 'in dreams behold the Hebrides'.

Compared with this, the oral answers crofters gave to questions in 1883 about what was then their present way of life have become a particularly valuable source of information. The Royal Commission, chaired by Lord Napier, asked the questions. Set up to inquire into the conditions of the crofters, the Royal Commission's members travelled round the Highlands to talk to them, something which had never been done before. It held meetings in sixty-one different places, going on for more than one day in ten of them, and listened to what 775 different people had to say. Most of the crofters in the west spoke in Gaelic. The Commission had every word they said translated, if necessary, written down in shorthand and sent to Neill and Co., Old Fishmarket, in the High Street of Edinburgh to be printed for presentation to Parliament and sale to the public on 28th April, 1884. In addition to their own Report and another five hundred pages of written evidence submitted to them, they printed 3,375 pages of oral answers to 46,750 questions, placing on record everything the crofters and other witnesses had to say. This is something else which, in the Highlands and Islands at least, had never been done before.

Crofter with a caschrom and his wife planting potatoes at Sconser in Skye in 1890 — note the creel and heaps of seaweed manure.

There must be few of us today who know anything at all about what our great-great-grandfathers thought or felt or said on any subject, yet here we have the words uttered by hundreds of ordinary men from Baltasound in Shetland to Tarbert on Loch Fyne, men who had been chosen by their fellows to speak for them on their conditions as crofters and who, but for this Royal Commission, would have passed away, unrecorded in the pages of history. Happily they were not required to confine their remarks to grievances about the land and their landlords, but were often encouraged to speak freely about their lives and experiences. As a result, they gave details about their methods of farming and fishing, their stock and their crops, seasonal work and other work, their homes, their food and their fuel, family relationships, their community the township and, all too frequently, unfortunately, their poverty. What they said as individuals could be of interest to people searching for their ancestors: collectively their testimony is a uniquely precious body of evidence about crofting as a way of life which deserves to be better known.

In recent years, several writers have written about the origins of crofting, the pressures of clearance for large-scale sheep farming and deer forests on the condition of the crofters, their resistance and their struggle to regain the land. The aim in this book is different — it is to go round the Highlands again with this Royal Commission, meet some of the outstanding personalities who spoke and, using their own words wherever possible, discover what they thought crofting life was really like a century ago. The men who feature here have not been chosen for any part they played in the land agitation in the 1880s, but for the vividness of their descriptions of their own lives or some aspect of crofting. Certain liberties have been taken: leaving out less essential parts, changing the order of topics occasionally, and running their answers to successive questions together to allow their accounts to flow in a more interesting way. In a few cases, this may give the impression that they gave evidence more willingly than they did on the day but care has been taken to be faithful to their testimony and not distort the meaning of what they said.

The illustrations, mostly photographs including some which well known photographers like George Washington Wilson of Aberdeen and James Valentine of Dundee took in the 1880s, are a very important part of the book. This was the time when these men, after years of concentrating on the outstanding views of Highland scenery which they knew visitors would buy, were beginning to take pictures of the people going about their everyday work as well. One reason for them making the change could easily be the interest in the crofters which this inquiry aroused. The photographs which appear here have been carefully chosen to complement the oral evidence and have been placed where they help to bring to life in picture form some aspect of their lives that the crofters are describing.

Notice to be posted on church doors etc., 1883.

V. R.

ROYAL COMMISSION.—Highlands and Islands.

NOTICE.

INTIMATION IS HEREBY MADE

That the **ROYAL COMMISSIONERS** intend to hold a Meeting for the purposes of their inquiry, at

on the   of   at 11 o'clock.

The Inhabitants are requested to elect Delegates for Examination before the Commission. The names of Persons thus selected should be communicated without unnecessary delay, to the 'Secretary to the Commission (Highlands and Islands), Parliament Square, Edinburgh.'

MORRISON & GIBB, EDINBURGH, PRINTERS TO H.M. STATIONERY OFFICE.

Stone erected in 1982 to mark the centenary of 'The Battle of the Braes'.

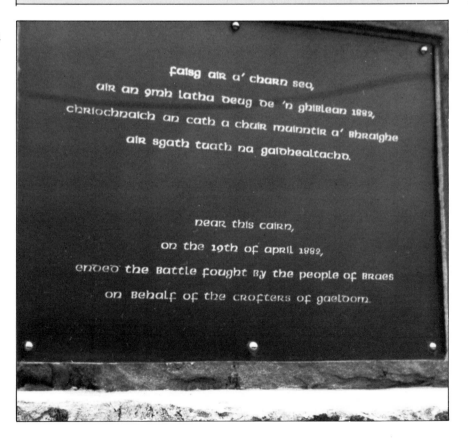

faisg air a' charn seo,
air an 9mh latha deug de 'n ghiblean 1882,
chriochnaich an cath a chuir muinntir a' bhraighe
air sgath tuath na gaidhealtachd.

near this cairn,
on the 19th of april 1882,
ended the battle fought by the people of braes
on behalf of the crofters of gaeldom

Go Listen to the Crofters

Sir William Harcourt, Home Secretary in Gladstone's Liberal Government, announced in the House of Commons on 19th March, 1883 that he was setting up a Royal Commission. Its purpose was 'to inquire into the conditions of the crofters and cottars in the Highlands and Islands of Scotland' and everything concerning them. The powers it was given were equally wide — to call any witness, to see any document and to visit any place it wished in order to acquire the fullest information possible. Clearly, to carry out this task properly, the Royal Commission was intended to go about the Highlands and listen to the crofters.

Looking back

The Home Secretary's announcement showed that the Government wished to tread the path of conciliation if it could and avoid the kind of violence in the Highlands which Ireland had experienced. It was now over sixty years since the Sutherland clearances, and thirty years since the great exodus following the potato famine in 1846 and the decline of the kelp industry, when people left the Islands, Skye and Mull, Lewis and Harris, the Uists and Barra, and the western seaboard from Wester Ross to Kintyre as emigrants bound for Canada, the United States and occasionally Australia. Probably about 60,000 went away between 1846 and 1861. Great numbers left places like Glenelg, Knoydart and Morvern on the mainland and some islands like Tiree and Coll, whereas towns like Stornoway and the north-east burghs grew in size and such was the natural increase, noticeable particularly in Lewis, that population in the Highlands and Islands overall fell by no more than 12,000 between 1861 and '81. The Highlands remained quiet, though crofters were finding the problem of feeding a growing family from little land becoming more and more difficult to resolve, while several landowners solved their problem, maintaining their income from the land, by turning sheep farms into deer forests and cashing in on the craze for deer stalking.

Then suddenly, it seemed law and order had broken down in Skye and there were places, notably the Braes in the east and Glendale in the north-west, where policemen in their usual island numbers dared not go. In an incident in 1882 which became known as 'The Battle of the Braes', fifty policemen who had been brought specially from Glasgow had to draw their batons and charge, to break through a crowd of crofters, both men and women, who were surrounding them and hurling stones at them. The grievance of the Braes crofters was the loss of their traditional hill pasture on Ben Lee behind their townships. When they asked for it back and were refused, they staged a rent strike, and burned the summonses the sheriff officer was trying to serve on them for being in arrears. The Glasgow police had come to try to arrest the five leaders in this mass defiance of the law. Afterwards, the Braes crofters put their cattle back on their old grazings on Ben Lee. Through the influence of Lochiel, Lord Macdonald the landlord, was persuaded to give them back their grazings to avoid the risk of troops being brought in. The crofters had won but at a price, the imposition of a fairly high rent for what they had previously regarded as their own. Still they were seen to have won a great victory because they had stood together and resisted violently when policemen were imported from the city to execute the laws.

The Glendale men whose crofts were small, on being refused the lease of the neighbouring sheep farm of Waterstein after Dr Nicol Martin gave it up, also refused to pay rent and drove their sheep up to graze on the pastures they wanted at Waterstein. They were so determined as a community that even orders against their leaders from the Court of Session in Edinburgh could not be enforced. Having armed themselves with sticks and other weapons, the Glendale crofters had driven the police out of their glen. The sheriffs of Skye and Inverness-shire recommended sending in troops to reinforce the police. The leaders must be arrested and brought to justice, they argued: that was the only way to show people that the law had to be obeyed. Unfortunately for the advocates of the use of military force, discontent was not a malady restricted to Skyemen. Crofters in Barra had their eyes on greener pastures over on Vatersay which they tried for when the lease of its sheep farm ran out, and others in Lewis living close to a deer forest were asking their landlord to give them a fairer share of the land. Getting the Glendale leaders to recognise the rule of law and present themselves before the Court of Session in Edinburgh was achieved in the end, not by force but by persuasion. The agent who arranged it was Malcolm MacNeill, a Gaelic-speaker whose official job made him responsible for the relief of the poor in the west Highlands. The men would not go on the gunboat *Jackal* on which MacNeill had arrived in Skye: they chose to go by themselves on David MacBrayne's steamer *Dunara Castle*. This was a victory for tact and commonsense. Three of them were sentenced on 16th March to two months imprisonment and 'in the course of the afternoon they were conveyed in a cab to the Calton Jail'. The sentence came as a shock to their supporters in Skye but when the news about this Royal Commission to look into the whole question of the crofters and the land broke a day or two later, they welcomed it as an achievement which reflected credit on their heroes, 'the Glendale martyrs'. In fact law-breaking actions by crofters in several places had combined to compel an unwilling Government to take this step. The Home Secretary, whose decision it was, preferred it to running the risk of sending in troops.

His announcement was particularly pleasing to Charles Fraser MacKintosh. He was the Liberal MP for the Inverness Burghs which he had represented since 1874. He was a lawyer and owner of a small estate near Inverness who combined a deep concern for his fellow Highlanders with his interest in their history and the Gaelic language. He had watched the pressure for a Royal Commission increasing over the last five or six years, only to be turned down again and again by the Government. That winter, 1882–83, which had seen great distress among the Skye crofters following the failure of their potato crop and their disappointingly low earnings at the east coast fishing, he tried again. He persuaded twenty other Scottish Liberal MPs, including some who had shown no interest in the voteless crofters before, to join him in sending a memorial to the Home Secretary asking for a Royal Commission. Not only was he hearing that there was to be one at last, but also that he was to be one of its members.

Lord Napier and Ettrick, the only one of the people appointed who was not a Highlander, was to be chairman; two of the members were big landowners in the Highlands, Donald Cameron of Lochiel, Conservative MP for Inverness-shire and owner of 110,000 acres in the county, and Sir Kenneth MacKenzie of Gairloch who owned 164,000 acres in Ross-shire and had recently been chief of the Gaelic Society of Inverness; and the other two were Alexander Nicolson, sheriff of Kirkcudbright but a native of Skye, first to climb Sgurr Alasdair, named after him in the Cuillins, and a collector of Gaelic proverbs, and Donald MacKinnon, a Colonsay man who had just become the first Professor of Celtic in Edinburgh University. Malcolm MacNeill, recently seen to be acceptable to the crofters by prevailing on the Glendale men to stand trial, moved over temporarily from his post with the Board of Supervision for the Relief of the Poor to become secretary of the Royal Commission at the same salary (£400 a year). Son of the laird of Colonsay, Malcolm MacNeill was also the nephew of Sir John MacNeill who had carried out an earlier enquiry in the Western Highlands and Islands on the Relief of the Poor in 1851.

Ridges in the landscape still show how intensively the land in Glendale, Skye was once cultivated.

In a notable scoop, *The Scotsman* printed these names in Edinburgh two days before the Home Secretary announced them in London. The paper highly approved of the selection — its independent chairman, 'two excellent landlords', the MP (Fraser MacKintosh) who had shown interest in the welfare of the crofters, three Gaelic speakers who would be, it assumed, sympathetic to the crofters' cause. One of the landlords, Sir Kenneth MacKenzie, agreed to serve after stating that in his opinion landowners ought not to be on the Commission at all, while in Parliament one critic regretted the absence of anyone to represent the crofter class. Alexander MacKenzie of Inverness, the author of *The Highland Clearances* (1881), who claimed the idea of a Royal Commission was originally his and whom Fraser MacKintosh had heard on the subject at a meeting of the Gaelic Society of Inverness back in 1877, thought the crofters could expect little from this one since all its members except one, Professor MacKinnon, were landlords or sons of landlords. The Highland Land Law Reform Association, which Highlanders in London had recently established, also entertained little hope that the Commission's report would be favourable to the crofters but it did all it could to help them to organise branches of the Association in their own areas and planned to send enthusiasts like Alexander MacKenzie to encourage the crofters to speak out and 'to guide and direct witnesses in preparing their evidence'.

Looking forward

The Royal Commission lost no time in setting about its task. All the members were present at the first meeting in Parliament Square, Edinburgh on Saturday, 31st March, and, two of them being lawyers, they began by defining their terms. For the purposes of their enquiry, they decided that a *crofter* was a person holding land for agricultural or pastoral purposes, individually or in common, directly from a proprietor at an annual rent of not more than £30. A *cottar*, on the other hand, was the occupier of a house at a rent of not more than £2 a year, who held no land or grazing rights from the proprietor. A *township* they defined as a district or group of crofter-holdings, called by a separate name, and the area they were to examine, *the Highlands and Islands of Scotland*, they held to extend over seven counties — Argyll, Inverness-shire, Ross and Cromarty, Sutherland, Caithness, Orkney and Shetland.

They proposed to acquire the information they thought they would need in two main ways: by holding meetings in different places to listen to oral evidence from crofters and others, and secondly by requiring each landowner to supply written evidence on printed forms about all the crofters and cottars he had on his estate. Their first meetings would be in Skye, where most of the troubles had been in the past year, starting at Braes on 8th May. Notices were to go to the schoolmaster of Braes and to all the ministers of Portree giving them the details and inviting the people to choose delegates to speak for them. Similar arrangements were made for meetings in Skye every day except Sunday for the next ten days. Meetings, they decided, were to be open to the public, including newspaper reporters but, the Lord Advocate advised them, they did not have the power to require witnesses to give evidence on oath. The Commissioners were to travel from place to place in a vessel which the Admiralty would supply. This turned out to be HMS *Lively*, a fast despatch boat which had carried supplies to relieve people who were suffering from famine in different parts of Ireland in 1881. It had a crew of over seventy under Commander A.A.C. Parr. Soon the newspapermen were asking if they could travel on her too, but this was not allowed, except for short journeys.

The Lively.

The Return about the crofters which each estate was expected to provide was intended to record a great deal of factual information — each crofter's name, the number of families living on each croft, the number of houses on the croft and the total number of people; the rent and any other dues, such as roadwork, which were expected from him; the area of arable land he had, the area of pasture; the number of horses, cows, calves, sheep he was allowed, known as his *summing* (souming); and the number he actually did have. The other Return, about the cottars, again asked for their names, whether or not their house was on someone's croft, whether they paid rent and to whom, and what their occupations were.

Factor's letter and proof that the Glendale people would not give the information he needed.

This was a kind of census. Although it did not ask for the names of all the other members of each household, as the official Population Census did, it did involve recording the measurements of each plot of land, counting the houses and animals, and even noting the ages of the cattle, and whereas completing the official Census return is the responsibility of each householder, all this information was to come from the estate owner or his factor. For a large estate like Lord MacDonald's on Skye where there were 892 crofters and 95 cottars and their families, it required days and nights of laborious work and soon factors were raising the question, 'Who is going to pay?'

To handle all the paper which was about to come flowing in, the Royal Commission appointed Robert Holden as chief clerk. He had been serving a similar body, the City of London Livery Companies Commission, whose work was coming to an end. It was hoped to appoint two more clerks, but the Treasury blocked this, seeing it as an example of empire-building. J. Irvine Smith, who had experience as shorthand writer to several Commissions and for the Crown in criminal cases in the High Court, was appointed to go with them as their shorthand writer, and they were allowed a messenger, Sergeant Peter Cunningham. Captain John MacDonald of Tobermory came highly recommended by yacht owners and the commander of HMS *Jackal* for his remarkable knowledge of western harbours and his skill at all hours and in all weathers to act as pilot on the *Lively*. Then the Post Office supplied a team of telegraphists to keep them in touch with London and the outside world. Anyone would think they were off to darkest Africa!

To deal with communities in the Highlands as small as townships which they would have to identify, good maps were essential. When the Secretary asked the Ordnance Survey to provide one-inch maps of the counties they were investigating, he received sheets covering the whole of Scotland, except for the west coast from Strome Ferry to Tarbert Loch Fyne and the islands off the coast, which had not yet been printed. Sadly, the area for which no maps were available included Skye where the Royal Commission was to begin its enquiry! The Ordnance Survey, however, promised to send the other maps 'in an unfinished state as soon as they can be printed'. The other source of information members hoped for was a good supply of newspapers while at sea. They asked for a dozen, ranging through the Glasgow titles, *The News*, *The Herald* and *The Mail* over to *The Scotsman* and from *The Times* to *The Spectator* and *The Pall Mall Gazette*! They were told politely, but no less firmly, that 'one paper (*Times* usually) is a recognised charge on public funds'. That paper and the Secretary's *Scotsman* which he paid for himself were all they had to look forward to at each port of call.

Since MPs have other duties, the full Royal Commission did not meet again until they were on board the *Lively* in Portree Bay on 7th May, but they did appoint Lord Napier, Sheriff Nicolson and Professor MacKinnon to act as a committee to cope with the early flow of business. Lord Napier, a Privy Councillor, was a landowner with 7,000 acres in Selkirkshire, and a retired diplomat. He had spent his life in the diplomatic service, having been Minister to the United States before the American Civil War, Ambassador to Russia during it, and then Governor of Madras in India, and for a short time, acting Viceroy. Back in Britain, he had shown an interest in social and educational questions and served as chairman of the London School Board. He was an able, kindly man, good at dealing with people, and with an immense capacity for work, as his team was beginning to discover.

Memorial to Lord Napier in Ettrick Kirk, Selkirkshire.

Meanwhile in the north, Alexander MacKenzie set out to travel round districts of the Highlands, Skye, Barra and the Uists making speeches ahead of the Royal Commission. So did John Murdoch, a retired exciseman and editor of *The Highlander* until it ceased publication in 1881, who intended to cover Harris and Lewis. Murdoch, always in a kilt, had become a well known public speaker who campaigned vigorously on Irish and Highland causes. 'Outside agitators', Alexander MacDonald, factor for most of the Skye estates, called them. They were coming, he said, to school the crofters into telling the Commission 'that what they wanted were larger holdings at fair rents with security of tenure'. Murdoch had, in fact, been impressed by how successful the Irish Land League had been, through using tactics of rent strikes and boycotts, and worse, against landlords. In 1881, tenants of land in Ireland had won from Gladstone a Land Act which granted them 'the three F's' — fair rents, fixity of tenure and free sale (or compensation for improvements they made themselves). Disturbances in Ireland had started earlier than in the Highlands and had been on a much more extensive scale but the rights that Irish peasants had achieved so recently were exactly what Highland crofters, when they were asked, said they wanted too.

Alexander MacKenzie was later to deny that he ever wrote or dictated a single word of any statement which any community submitted to the Commission. Even if this is true, it is likely that, since many of the statements must have been written by local people soon after hearing a speech by him or John Murdoch, these two men had considerable influence. The frequency with which 'the three F's' were to be recited before the Royal Commission in very different places lends support to this view. Hearing these phrases early, on the Royal Commission's second day in Skye, Cameron of Lochiel was to emphasise that they had come to hear each crofter speak his own thoughts on his conditions of life:

'We do not want the mere catch words "fixity of tenure" and "compensation for improvements", but we want, being on the spot here, to find out exactly what it is you want'.

Fortunately they were to find a great number were ready to respond in that spirit.

Skyemen and the Difficulties of Crofting

In the row of churches in Portree on Sunday, 6th May, 1883, all the ministers prayed for the Commissioners. They asked God that they might bring peace and happiness back to the island, and James Reid, the Free Church minister went further, expressing the hope that 'the yoke of oppression would be broken where it existed'. That afternoon, the naval vessel *Lively* arrived from Oban and anchored in the bay. On board were four members of the Royal Commission: one lord, the chairman, Lord Napier; one clan chief, Donald Cameron of Lochiel; one sheriff, Alexander Nicolson; and one professor, Donald MacKinnon, Professor of Celtic in Edinburgh. The other two members, Sir Kenneth MacKenzie of Gairloch and Charles Fraser MacKintosh, were soon to join them to start their great enquiry.

People in Portree talked of little else. The sight of the *Lively*, though a lightly armed ship, was a sign of Government presence. It was nearly a month since the notices about the meetings appeared, like Luther's ninety-five theses at Wittenberg, nailed on the church doors in Portree. These gave the time and place of the first meeting at the Braes (11 o'clock on 8th May in the old school at Ollach) and told people to choose delegates to put their case from among their fellows in each township. But would the crofters take the risk and speak up, bearing in mind what the factors and the law might do? They all knew that three Glendale crofters were still in Calton Prison and fresh in their minds was 'The Battle of the Braes' which happened here only a year ago. People came from far and near to the Royal Commission's first meeting at Ollach, seven miles south of Portree, and two hundred of them managed to squeeze into the church used as a schoolroom.

Church used as a school at Upper Ollach where the Royal Commission's first meeting was held.

Angus Stewart for the Braes crofters

Angus Stewart, aged 40, a crofter's son, one of seven people living in his father's house at Peinchorran where the little crofts ran down to the shore, was the first witness. He began by making two requests in broken English. The first, to be examined in Gaelic, was granted immediately and Dugald MacLachlan, bank agent and sheriff-clerk depute, began to act as interpreter. Then he asked for an assurance that he would not be evicted by the landlord or the factor for what he had to say. Otherwise, he said, 'I would not have a fire in my house at Whitsunday'. The landlord, Lord MacDonald, was not present. Alexander MacDonald, his factor, tried hard to avoid giving a direct answer. Then when he was reminded that this Royal Commission could not carry out its investigation thoroughly if witnesses felt that giving evidence freely would endanger their future, he relented and at last gave the assurance that nothing would ever be done prejudicial to him or his family for anything he might say that day.

Sheriff Court House, Portree, scene of its longest meeting.

Angus Stewart then put his case:

'The principal thing we complain of is our poverty. The smallness of our holdings and the poor quality of the land is what has caused our poverty, and the way in which the poor crofters are huddled together, and the best part of the land devoted to deer forests and big farms. The people cannot take a crop out of the ground; it does not yield crops to them. It is a great hardship that all our earnings at the fishing we have to put into meal for the support of our families. With land which has been cropped continuously for the past thirty years, within my own memory, we cannot get back out of the ground two-thirds of what we put into it. I do not mean that is so every year. The year before last we only had one and a half bushel over and above what we actually put in. We cannot leave any part of our cultivated ground out of cultivation. What would we cultivate if we were to leave half of it out? What would feed the cattle for us?

'The remedy throughout the island of Skye is easy to supply — give us land out of the plenty that there is about for cultivation. Give us land at a suitable rent — at a rent within our power to pay.

'You ask where this land lies? There are thirty *tacks* (farms on lease) in the Isle of Skye and many of these are capable of supporting hundreds of families in comfort. They surround us, Scorrybreck, Glenvarigil, Corrie, Broadford, and all the way down to the Point of Sleat. I want the people to migrate to land now occupied by large farmers. I cannot say how far the people would wish to move. I, at any rate, would go any distance to get good land, and I think my neighbours would. Unless we can get this, poverty will not be got out of Skye forever. We will always need a Joseph in the south to send us seed (corn).

'It is our being deprived of the hill pasture of Ben Lee which has thrown us back the past number of years. Though the hill of Ben Lee was taken from us 16 or 17 years ago, no reduction was made in our rents'.

'We got Ben Lee back last winter', Angus Stewart explained, 'but although it was part of our holdings in time past, we now have to pay £74,15s. for it. We claim the sum is too large. We offered to pay rent because there was blood shed about it and because we were sorely threatened by the law of the land. We offered a rent for peace's sake and there was a gentleman who offered to put a thousand pounds aside in order to make peace between Lord MacDonald and the crofters, and most of us thought this thousand pounds would be ours for the stocking of the hill but it was not. Most of us have not been able to stock the hill, except for a few sheep the people have grazing on it. Unless we get help outside, in some other way, I don't see how we can do it.

Boggy land still with Ben Lee behind at Peinchorran where in Angus Stewart's croft his descendant, Sorley MacLean, the great Gaelic poet, lives now.

'My father used to be able to keep four cows generally and nine or ten sheep on the hill. Some years there might have been a stirk, other years none, and some years we might have two stirks. In my grandfather's time, there were five tenants in Peinchorran and now there are twenty-six or twenty-seven. When the land is sub-divided, the new crofter has to build his own house. May the Lord look upon you, he gets no help! I have myself had to go to the deer forest to steal rushes — to steal the wherewith to thatch our houses. I went in the daytime and was caught by the gamekeeper, across in Sconser, and I had to give him part of what I had. It is across in Raasay that we get our timber for our houses, and to make the creels for us to carry the manure for cultivation to our ground and the crooked spade for tilling the ground. We get it all from Raasay.

'I cannot tell the exact acreage of my father's croft but I can say there is not one acre of it worth cultivating or worth putting seed into. It is rocky, mossy ground. I might catch a deer in it, it is so boggy. Other parts of it are as hard as adamant.

'I think small tenants like us would be much better in every way immediately under the Government. I think the land laws should be altered. I mean the proprietors should be replaced by the Government. The Queen should be our landlord'.

This must have been all too much for Alexander MacDonald, the factor, sitting listening in the schoolroom. He acted for the present proprietor and his version of the number of crofts was that there had been 13 crofts in 1811, and there were still 13, although they had since been sub-divided. During the break after Angus Stewart had been examined, the two of them must have exchanged words at the very least, as Malcolm MacNeill, the Secretary discovered when he received this terse note:

'During the interval our factor cursed me to the face
angus stewart, Delegte.'

As a result, the factor felt obliged to make this further statement in public, guaranteeing the immunity of witnesses:

'I wish to say that witnesses have the very fullest opportunity of saying whatever they choose, true or false— I leave it to themselves — without fear of anything whatever from anybody'.

Donald Nicolson of Solitote on being evicted:

I am 78 years old. I had a croft at Totescore (north of Uig), but it was taken from me. Now I am only going from house to house. My rent was £7,10s. and it was doubled at once, and another pound was added. I did not refuse to pay the double rent, but I declined to pay the extra pound. I then got warning. When the summer came, the officer came and ejected me. He put everything I had out of the house. I was only wanting payment for my houses (outhouses) and then I would go. The doors were locked against me.

'The tacksman told the rest of the crofters that anyone who would open door to me would be treated the same way as I was. Not one of them would let me into his house, they were so afraid. My son's wife was in with her two young children, and we were that night in the cart-shed, and our neighbours were afraid to let us in, and crying over us. The peats were locked up. We had not a fire to prepare a cake (an oatcake). There was plenty of meal outside, but we had not a fire to prepare it. I was staying in the stable during the summer. I could make only one bed in it. My daughter and my son's wife and the two children were sleeping in that bed, and I was sleeping on the stones.

'The Presbytery allowed me to enter the glebe. The factor then shut up my outhouses and I cannot enter them. It is Mr James Grant, the minister of the parish (Kilmuir) who is supporting me today. I earn nothing now, unless Mr Grant helps me. My family was scattered when I lost the place'.

The Commissioners were much impressed by old Donald, who like nearly all the Skye crofters was putting his case in Gaelic, and Sheriff Nicolson called him 'a brave old fellow'. But the factor's story was that Donald was a nuisance to his neighbours, through keeping too many horses and letting them stray all over the place. He had been warned and warned, and then he was turned out. When he went in again a decree was pronounced against him for the sum of £53,3s.2d. for damages and expenses.

'In December, I took off £25', said the factor, 'we did not want to be hard on the old man' but in fact, he and the sheriff-clerk depute, the only two lawyers practising in Skye, had acted together against this obstinate old man. This drove Sheriff Nicolson to observe, 'It is remarkable that a poor man in the Isle of Skye should be in circumstances in which both the practising agents in Skye may be in a position in which it is impossible for them to take up his case'.

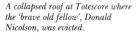

A collapsed roof at Totescore where the 'brave old fellow', Donald Nicolson, was evicted.

Donald MacLeod on small holdings and earlier evictions

In the school among the birch trees, at Torran in Raasay the
Commissioners listened to Donald MacLeod, who was also 78, talking
about earlier evictions:

'I have lived all my days in Kyle Rona and nine heads of families elected
me to speak. In my memory, it was five families who were in the
township, and today there are ten families. Not many were taken in from
other townships; it was the natural increase of the place. They were
dividing the lots to their sons'.

His own son, Charles, had the neighbouring croft to his, but they all
lived together, nine of them, in Donald's house.

'You ask me about the first eviction in the time of MacLeod of Raasay
himself — I don't remember that, but I remember Mr (George) Rainy
about thirty years ago clearing fourteen townships, and he made them
into a sheep farm which he had in his own hands. The people from
Castle, Screpidale, two Hallaigs (and eight other townships which he
named) went to other kingdoms — some to America, some to Australia,
and other places that they could think of. There were a great number of
people in the fourteen townships, hundreds, young and old. I am sure
there were a hundred in each of two of the townships. The townships
were altogether arable land capable of being ploughed. Now they are all
in the proprietor's hands and the only inhabitants of that land today are
rabbits and deer and sheep.

'All these clearings were not done in one year. I don't well remember
how long it was going on. The people Rainy cleared did not go of their
own accord. They were sorry to leave. They were weeping and wailing
and lamenting, taking handfuls of grass that was growing over the graves
of their families in the churchyard, as remembrances of their kindred.

'When the people went away, they weren't taken away in ships that
came here. They went by steamer to Glasgow. I don't know but the
landlord paid their passage. He was giving money to some to induce them
to go. He may have been giving a little clothes but it was not in his mind
to do them much good at all. He did not care where they went to, as long
as they left his estate'.

Angus Galbraith, the Free Church minister since 1867, said he'd been
told 97 families were cleared against their will at this time (1852–54) and
Alexander MacLennan, another old crofter from Eilean Fladda,
remembered being on the quay when the people were sent away:

'They were like lambs separated from their mothers', he said. 'There
was one old man there who said, "Should I go to Australia I may die on
my arrival; I should prefer to remain on Raasay but I must go".'

In a recent book *Raasay, a study in history*, R. Sharpe supports much of
the evidence old Donald MacLeod gave. The townships were not all
cleared at the same time: the Hallaigs were cleared later, in 1854. 125
people signed that they agreed to emigrate to Australia, although the
opinion of Angus Galbraith, the minister, was that most of them were sent
away against their will. In the end, 129 did go and the first stage of their
journey on 6th June was on board MacBrayne's *Chevalier*, a steamer, as
Donald MacLeod had said.

John MacCaskill on compulsory labour by cottars

'I am a cottar and shoemaker at Fernilea in Bracadale. The present
tacksman (leaseholder), Donald Colin Cameron of Talisker deprived the
cottars of the grazing for their cows, and took from us our peat mosses,
and gave us a bog which neither man nor beast made use of up to that
time. Then twice he brought ten or twelve more families of cottars into

Fernilea, and divided the existing holdings to make room for them. Seven of us have got grazing for a cow again.

'We have to attend the tacksman of Talisker on any day he requires us to work. When he's paying us, a strong man, should he be as strong as Samson, would get only 1s. a day and our women 6d. a day. I am a shoemaker, having learned the trade, and my brother also, and we would have to leave our work and would be losing our business for the sake of doing Talisker's work at 1s. a day. It is field work, sometimes three days a week in spring, summer and harvest — when field work is being done'.

When Cameron of Talisker was asked about it, he had this to say:

'The cottars are bound to work certain days, but I don't suppose there is a single cottar who has worked more than twenty days in the year. They get a shilling a day and their food — porridge and milk for breakfast, and flour scones and meat and broth or potatoes for dinner. They feed in my own kitchen with my own house servants.

'When I took the farm thirty-three years ago, the wages were one shilling a day to the men and food, and 6d. a day and food to the women, and it is the same now'.

Pressed by Lord Napier, he had to agree that wages had risen in the last thirty years and that a free labourer now might expect to be paid 50s. for twenty days work. The excuse he gave for not raising wages was, 'They never made a complaint to me, and they were willing to come'.

Norman Stewart of Valtos on high rents

It was in the schoolhouse at Uig that the Commission first heard that big increases in rent were a major cause of complaint. Old Donald Beaton, a crofter at Earlish on the Kilmuir estates belonging to Major Fraser of Newton in the county of Nairn, handed in two receipts, one for £3,17s.6d, which was a full year's rent in 1852, and another for £10,1s. for 1880. £9 of this was for the year's rent for the same land, 9s.9d. for poor rate, 6s. for school rates, 3s. for roads, and 2s.3d. interest. He admitted he'd had a reduction of £1 for the last year which had been a bad one but said he couldn't live paying the present rent with two cows, when he had to buy in feeding for them and his family.

They heard the same kind of story from Norman Stewart, a crofter and salmon fisher of Valtos on the same estate. He had four months work at home at the salmon until September and went away to get work at the beginning of winter until it was time for spring work on the croft.

'My rent is £7,10s. for half a croft, 3½ or 4 acres. On it I have two cows and a horse but no young cattle. I had seven or eight sheep but the sheep have gone entirely this year. The rents have been raised three times. The first was soon after Major Fraser came, about twenty-six years ago; my rent went up by more than £1. The next rise was ten years ago — five shillings for the doctor. The third rise was about six years ago — my rent went up from £4,14s. to £7,10s. altogether. The rents of all the Valtos people were raised in the same way.

'Yes, we complained to the factor. He asked us to try it for one year. We were paying it for two or three years until we refused to pay. The factor threatened to remove us altogether if we did not pay the increase. In the end we got a reduction of £1,2s.6d'.

Major Fraser wrote from Nairn that he could not appear before the Commission as he was unwell and could not travel and his doctor certified 'on soul and conscience' that this was so. His factor read a long statement from Major Fraser in which he agreed that there had been three rent increases, the third on the advice of a skilled farmer from Nairn, where farms are very different. Major Fraser claimed he had spent a great deal on roads to improve the estate and invested heavily in the Skye Railway.

Cross-examined by Sheriff Nicolson, the factor admitted first, 'that the rental of Major Fraser's estate had been greatly increased', then 'that it had been very nearly doubled' and finally 'that it has been the only estate in Skye on which the rent had been nearly doubled in so short a period'. He agreed that it was only within the last three or four years that tenants in Skye had ever raised their voices in complaint:

'It began at Kilmuir', he said, 'with the township of Valtos. The tenants alleged that the ground officer gave in for the summing of the township two cows more than the real number. When Major Fraser was satisfied that they were correct, he at once reduced the rent.

'That was the beginning of the crofters holding meetings and putting their heads together. I know that on Major Fraser's estate officers of the law at the time of the Valtos agitation were afraid to go there'.

John MacPherson of Glendale, a hero's return

Before landing in Skye the Commission was being pressed to hold a meeting in Glendale. Three letters with this message arrived from Skye, all in English, all word for word the same, each written and signed by a different crofter, but who dictated them we do not know. The Secretary replied that there would be a meeting, but postponed fixing a date until he knew when the three Glendale men would be released from the Calton Jail.

On Thursday 17th May two of them, Donald MacLeod and John Morrison returned to Dunvegan on the *Dunara Castle*. John MacPherson, travelling by rail via Inverness and Strome Ferry, was back in Skye before them and was carried shoulder-high through hundreds of cheering supporters into the Portree Hotel. 'The martyrs' were welcomed home in Skye.

The Free Church, Glendale, scene of crowded meetings in May 1883.

On the Saturday, white flags (made out of towels or sheets or handkerchiefs) fluttered on poles or fishing-rods beside every cottage as a sign of goodwill and, called by the sound of the horn (still in the possession of John MacPherson's family), close on 600 people crowded into the Free Church at Glendale. John MacPherson began by asking for the customary assurance of immunity, adding 'I got sixty-one days already for telling the truth, and asking for justice'. Clearly, he was playing in front of his home crowd. From the Return John Robertson the factor made on behalf of the landlords, the Trustees of MacPherson MacLeod, the Commission could learn no more than that he was the tenant of no. 6 croft at Lower Milovaig at a rent of £4,4s. and was allowed to keep 3 cows and 8 sheep. The Milovaig people having already refused to pay rents also refused to give the factor the details he needed for these forms. John

MacPherson provided the simple details of his life: He was 48, the son and grandson of crofters, and had been a crofter-fisherman for 28 years, married now with seven children, and still living in the same place. Although much of his evidence was on the land question, he was interesting also on people's work, their food and their homes:

'All the money we get is earned by people going south and getting wages, unless we sell a stirk. We are not home scarcely for a week with our earnings when we pay it over to the proprietors, and they are off to London and elsewhere abroad to spend it. Not a penny of it is spent on the place for which the rent is paid.

'My croft is about three acres of very shallow land. I have no horse. We and our wives do the ploughing and harrowing of our land, turning or tilling it with the caschrom, the most primitive mode of tilling, I believe, in existence.

'With more families sharing the hill pasture and cutting peats on it, hill grazing is scarce and people suffer badly. Instead of the milk they had formerly, now they have only treacle and tea to wash down the food. Our staple food is meal, potatoes, fish when it is got, our only drink being tea. On average, we consume sixteen bolls of south country meal, which costs us between £17 and £20. I don't count the number of hens we have at home, but I don't think it is more than five or six. If we had more, we would have to buy feeding for them from Glasgow and these places.

'A single Aberdeenshire cow would outweigh three of ours. When I was asked in the south country and said I kept three cows on the croft, they thought I was well off and that I was a gentleman. The amount of milk they give is very meagre, and all our feeding would not do justice to more than one cow. The food with which we winter our stirks we have to buy in Glasgow.

'Our dwelling houses are thatched with straw. As our crofts do not produce enough straw for fodder for the cattle as well as for thatch, and as we are prohibited from cutting rushes or pulling heather, our houses in rainy weather are most deplorable. Above our beds comes pattering down the rain, rendered dirty and black by the soot on the ceiling, and so the inmates of the beds have to look for shelter on the lee side of the house. Of the twenty houses there are only two in which the cattle are not under the same roof as the family'.

John MacPherson was the only witness the Commission had time to hear that day. Proceedings had started at 11 a.m. as usual and ended at 3 in the afternoon to give members the opportunity to look at the people's houses and explore the disputed pastures on Waterstein. Then they returned to their own temporary home, the *Lively*. Returning to land at Colbost on the Monday morning, they met girls on their way to catch the steamer, some with their luggage in pony carts, and others carrying their trunks on their backs. They were on their way to jobs in service in the south, clear evidence of how few opportunities there were for young people in Skye.

The Elgol people, their difficulties and hopes

The people of Elgol on the exposed west of Skye had chosen Donald MacKinnon, aged 45, and Norman Robertson, who was 71, to speak for them. They were both crofters: Donald was also a fisherman. Donald said there were forty-five crofting families paying rent at Elgol and seventeen cottar familes besides — close on 400 people living on poor land. They paid road money but they were three miles from the end of the nearest road. Beside them were two very big farms with only seven families on them. All this belonged to Alexander MacAllister of Strathaird, their landlord. They got no work from him, however, and it was a rough shore to fish from. They had to go away to the east coast or to Ireland for work at the fishing. Asked if he was born in Skye, Donald said he was, and added 'I am a Skyeman to my backbone'.

Cutting seaweed with sickles in Skye to be taken home by boat, 1890.

The school at Elgol built too close to the shore, the fishermen said in 1883, but still educating little Robertsons and MacKinnons today, and the bridge built when Elgol got its road.

The Return the proprietor completed on Elgol revealed three crofts held by different tenants all called Donald MacKinnon. One had four families on it, each with its own house, a total of 22 people; one with two families and two houses totalled 12 people; and the third had three families on it in three houses, adding up to 15 people. This was, of course, MacKinnon country. Four of the other crofts had tenants called Robertson, one of whom, Norman, described their lives at present and in times past and offered hope for the future:

'In our townships we have no peat moss. We get our peats from Mr Bower, the neighbouring tacksman, but many of the people do not have that privilege. We don't pay for them. His peat moss is quite far away, a mile from the man who is farthest from it.

'We have horses. There is a horse allowed to every full croft. Those who have land suitable for ploughing use the horses. Others have not been able to use a horse at all in cultivating their land. They use the caschrom.

'I am not a fisherman now. We seldom fish for cod and ling. Those who have nets go to the Loch Hourn herring fishing but there are not many in our township who have nets. They are not able to buy them. People would go more to the fishing if they had more nets. The south country people are spoiling the fishing in Loch Hourn — fishing it in daylight and trawling, and so spoiling it for the poor people — trawling even on the Sabbath day!

'Herrings were 2s.6d. to 18s. per cran last year. 2s.6d. is a very small price. If the poor people could salt them they could wait and get a better price for them. If they had money to buy barrels and salt, they themselves could sell the herring when they had cured them. But we have no means of curing them. If the steamers will not take them, perhaps a poor man will lose twelve crans or more, and then his nets along with them.

'I have not seen so much destitution as this season, for the last forty years — such want of food, not since the great potato famine of 1846. Many of us got relief from the Committee. Those who went to ask relief and needed it, got it. Many are still needy and didn't get it, but I don't think they asked for it.

'My memory can go back long before the potato disease. People had plenty of food then. They were making food from what they grew themselves — making meal of their own oats, and using their potatoes. When my father had the croft, he had fifty sheep at least. Now I don't believe there are more than two for each lot. Of course, in my father's time there were perhaps sixteen or seventeen paying rent and now there are forty-five. Some of the Keppoch people who would not go to Australia were settled down among us. That explains the increase partly at least.

'My idea of a fair comfortable croft would have a summing of four or five cows, forty or fifty sheep and a horse or two, and the arable needed to winter these cattle and horses would be ten or eleven acres. I would say a fair rent for that croft would be £8.

'A large number of the families in Elgol could not take crofts now, even if they got them, because they are too poor, but those who couldn't take such large crofts could take smaller ones. These people would need assistance also to stock them. But there is plenty of land in the country for the whole of them, if they got it. The land my grandfather had is in green rigs, marching with us, on the other side of the fence (the neighbouring sheep farm). If we could only get land we could work. We would be thankful to pay a fair rent for it'.

After that meeting the Commissioners and the Elgol people can hardly have expected that they would ever meet again. But at the beginning of August a fever epidemic broke out in Elgol and the Commission was instructed to return on the *North Star* to investigate. Twenty-five people, they discovered, were suffering from fever and three had died. The houses, some of which were described as being in a wretched condition, had been disinfected by the medical officer, who then caught the disease himself. The Commissioners did what they could, emphasising the need to isolate victims and leaving medical supplies and food.

Island of idleness or lack of opportunity?

Another Donald MacKinnon, the minister of Strath was the third generation of the same family who were ministers of this parish continuously for over a hundred years. He reckoned crofters were wrong if they imagined they could support their familes from the land alone because their crofts were so small:

'Crofters were never intended or expected to be self-sufficient farmers', he said, 'but working men with allotments. When crofting came to engross their whole time and attention, it is no cause of wonder that poverty has come. A very large majority of our male adult population spend from eight to nine months of the year in absolute idleness, and consequently in poverty'.

The Royal Commission had heard many witnesses, John MacPherson and Norman Stewart among them, who travelled far from Skye every year in order to get work and avoid idleness. It is true, however, that at home many crofters were inclined not to improve their crofts because they lacked security of tenure or else feared their rent would be raised if they did so. But they resented the implication that they were lazy. In the township of Digg on Staffin Bay where none of the crofters had a horse, one of them, Alexander Nicolson protested:

'Surrounded by sheep farms on every side of us, we have no place for sheep or a horse. Whenever we speak about a horse we will be advertised as lazy. Will you say "lazy man" to a people who carry 200 to 400 creels full of sea-weed every spring time to spread on the arable land?'

Magnificent and wild, the Cuillins seen from Elgol.

The kind of work he was defending required effort, but it was not the most productive way of working: he knew he'd have been more efficient if he'd had a horse. Employers on the mainland, like George Grant MacKay of Glengloy who was noted for making land more productive, found men from Skye very good workers, as long as they needed the money:

'Every Skye man I employ gets 2s.6d. a day and, being industrious, frugal, good men, they live on fourpence a day, and save the 2s.2d., every penny of it. They never spend a penny on drink, but go back to their families in Skye, and live in a dormant state till the 2s.2d. is done. Then they come and work for me again. At home as long as they have meal and potatoes they won't work.

'They are ready to take any employment: there are no better people than they are that way. They built a silo for silage for me, and they've done a good deal of road-making and planting. They're capital at anything. I always have a skilled man over them, never a Skye man'.

If the Royal Commission could give the crofters security of tenure, the men would then have an incentive to improve their crofts; and if they were to gain more land they could feed their families better and farm with a higher aim than selling a stirk merely because they needed the money to pay the rent. As yet Skye offered far too few alternative occupations, little in the way of public works, or fishing in big boats owned by local firms, or manufacturing industry, other than Talisker distillery where a small number of workers only were needed to produce a valuable malt whisky, using imported barley. The only local materials required were peat and water. Since tourism also was still in its infancy, most men and young people had little option but to leave the island in summer to try to find work.

Lord Napier and his Commission spent fifteen busy days in Skye where they won respect because they showed they were willing to listen sympathetically at very long meetings. Sittings of seven and a half to eight hours a day were common and their last one, in Portree, went on for more than ten hours!

People of the Long Island
Barra and the Uists

Barra

On 26th May, the Royal Commission crossed over to Barra. They were arriving at the south end of the long string of islands, stretching to the Butt of Lewis a hundred and thirty miles away, called the Long Island or the Outer Hebrides. When the *Lively* entered Castlebay, the great natural harbour round Kisimul Castle, old home of the chiefs of MacNeill, she was dressed overall with flags in honour of the Queen's birthday, which was actually two days earlier. The Barra herring season was at its height, with 350 fishing boats, nearly all from the north-east ports, sailing in with their catches. All along the shore were the curers' huts and bothies, and barrels by the hundred to be filled with salt herrings.

Because of their meeting in the new schoolroom, the school log-book records that the children were given a holiday for the day. The Commissioners learned how much the herring fishing meant to the local people, even although only eight of the boats engaged actually belonged to Barra. John MacKinnon, formerly a crofter in Tangusdale, told them he was better off curing fish for Mr MacNeill, a local merchant, in summer and earning 2s. and sometimes 2s.6d. a day, and doing jobs about his house in winter for 1s.6d. a day. One of his daughters went away to the east coast fishing each year, and the other two helped her when the Barra fishing was on. Another man, a cottar, made a living finding women to work for the curers, who needed three women to gut and salt the herrings caught by each boat. He couldn't say that the women liked the work, only that 'they were very ready to accept it'.

Castlebay school where the Commission met in 1883, still in use in 1983 as the children's bicycles show.

Castlebay, Barra about 1910 with Kisimul Castle surrounded by east coast boats.

Thirty-three curers were at Castlebay for the season and one of them was Thomas Ross from Burghead on the Moray Firth. According to him, each crew from the north-east brought one or two women with them who, as he put it, 'generally belong to the men as a rule' (at least to their families). They engaged most of the women workers they needed from the people on the island. The women received £1 of earnest (an advance on being engaged) and eight pence for every barrel they filled, giving them about £3 for the season if the fishing was good, or 50s. on an average. They were always paid in money, never in goods.

Fishing boats there today.

The time for the Barra fishing was from 15th or 20th May to 23rd June, when the north-east boats would take on one or two Barra men each to make up their crews and pay them £5 to £7 and their food on board. The curers were usually at Castlebay longer, for about eight weeks as a rule, and most of the herrings sent away from Barra were bound for Baltic ports, mainly for the Russian market. Although the time this seasonal paid work lasted was short, it was important to families in Barra, where there were almost no other opportunities to earn money for working at home and undoubtedly it helped to keep a large population on the island.

Barra was sold by Roderick MacNeill in 1838 and, like South Uist and Benbecula in the Clanranald estate, it had passed into the hands of Col. Gordon of Cluny in Aberdeenshire by 1841. The Commissioners knew from the factor's Returns that there were 205 crofting families in Barra, and 39 cottars' families. One of the crofters, 40-year-old Michael Buchanan of Borve who is remembered locally as having learned seven languages at Arbuckle's school in Craigston, told them:

'The fishing industry is a great help, combined with that of land. When I don't get to sea, if I have some land I still have something to support me. A fisherman should have about seven acres to keep a cow and a horse, with potato ground. A cow is very necessary for milk, where young children are brought up. The peats for fuel here are in inaccessible patches of moss land now and people require a pony to carry home their peats. People do not go about here as they do on the east coast with a cart selling peats or a pennyworth of milk or half a hundredweight of coal. Therefore, the fisherman needs to have land.

'We live in thatched cottages and have to labour twelve days for Dr MacGillivray, the tacksman (of Eoligarry in the north which covered a third of Barra), for two small cart-loads of bent grass to thatch our houses. (Dr MacGillivray said he was exaggerating: it was 4s. or 4 short days' work a cartload). There is heather enough for thatching: I never heard any labour being asked in return for the heather.

'I also say that Dr MacGillivray takes sixty days' labour on an average for an acre of land for planting potatoes. Each person takes the planting of a barrel of potatoes, and we calculate an acre to plant about eight barrels. The value of a day's labour among the big farmers is a shilling, so Dr MacGillivray gets at the rate of £3 an acre. The return we get from one barrel is eight barrels, or ten or twelve in a good year, and some years hardly double the seed we put in'.

The factor, Ronald MacDonald of Aberdeen declared that Michael Buchanan was an unreliable witness whose main occupation had been going about preaching discontent among the people, and said no one

Michael Buchanan's Borve, a thatched township in 1883, its school at Craigston in the background left and Free Church on the right still in use today.

connected with the estate paid any attention to him. Michael told how they tried to rent the island of Vatersay, south of Barra:

'When Vatersay was advertised in the newspapers to be let, the inhabitants of Glen and Castlebay wanted it, and three men went to see the chief factor at Aberdeen. Castlebay is very rocky and rugged and its green patches are very bleak, barren and sterile ground. The land on Vatersay is the finest on the island. They wanted to go and live there' (but they did not get it).

South Uist

Alexander MacNeil, who was eighty now and had half a croft at Smerclett in the south, explained how important making *kelp* (fertiliser rich in potash made by burning seaweed) once was to the crofters:

'My father always paid his rent by kelp. No, we did not cut the weed for the proprietor; we ourselves manufactured the kelp. We never sold a pound of it but to the proprietor. We were paid according to the weight delivered over to him, so much per ton, £2,10s., £2, and sometimes £3 per ton. I think the proprietor, Lady Gordon Cathcart, does not care to continue this kelp manufacture now, because it does not pay. Latterly, the price fell very much.

'When I was young no one had to leave the country to labour. Instead of going south they used to labour at kelp at home; but now in the absence of the kelp industry, they are obliged to run away to the east country, or wherever they can get employment.

'We are constantly growing poorer. When my father had a (whole) croft for himself, he never bought a pound of meal, and in those days the potatoes would be in heaps. People are not half as cheerful now: they cannot be happy when they are hungry'.

Potatoes growing on lazybeds at Lochboisdale.

The Commission learned from John MacKay, an old crofter of Kilpheder, west of Lochboisdale that he used to be able to make four or five tons of kelp by himself when he was young, and get from £2,10s. a ton. That kept him from getting into arrears with his rent, and helped him to buy food but now that source of income had gone. Then he recalled the last of the forced emigrations to Canada, which took place in August 1851 and described some of the incidents he remembered:

'I saw a policeman chasing a man down the *machair* (sandy plain on the

Atlantic side) towards Askernish to catch him in order to send him on board an emigrant ship lying in Loch Boisdale. That man was Donald Smith. I saw another man who lay down on his face and nose, hiding himself from the policeman, and the policeman getting a dog to search for this missing man. The dog did not discover him, but he was afterwards discovered all the same. He had got into the trench of a *lazy-bed* (a potato bed with a trench on each side for drainage). He was Lachlan MacDonald, he was over twenty years old and he was taken off. His brother also went away at the same time, and there's a nephew here today.

'I have no doubt there were many other cruelties in the course of these evictions. I myself was in charge of a squad of men working on a road when Mr Chisholm and Murdoch McLennan, two tacksmen wanting to clear the country for themselves, wished me to go to Locheynort to bring people out of their homes to be sent out in an emigrant ship. I told them, "I am in charge of a squad of men working upon these roads, paid by the proprietor. I have nothing to do with searching houses or taking men out of them. If you have constables, send them". They went away and they did send them.

'That was the last forcible eviction on these estates. Five emigrant ships left Lochboisdale. All the people on board were from the Gordon estates from Benbecula to Barra Head. Most of their land was added to the big farms'.

Benbecula

One of the many MacDonalds they listened to was old John MacDonald in the schoolroom at Torlum. He was 75 and represented seventeen or eighteen crofters in Gramisdale in the north of the island. He told them what it was like to be poor in Benbecula in 1883:

'The vast majority of the people are as poor as it is possible for them to be. The children of school age who ought to be attending school are sent out to the North Ford to gather cockles for food. I almost never travel: it is very seldom, indeed, that I go on any journey from home. There is no one in my township sufficiently well off to pay for a newspaper (*The Scotsman* at the time cost 1d) to know what is going on outside the island. I don't know who the Prime Minister is, but I understand the member for the county (of Inverness) is Lochiel'.

This raised a laugh and a cheer, which he shared with Lochiel, one of the members of the Royal Commission sitting listening to him.

North Uist

For the meeting in the Free Church at Locheport, the pilot brought the *Lively* right up the long winding loch past the cottages on the south side where white flags were fluttering in welcome. John Morrison who was 60 told how his people came to be at Locheport:

'Thirty-two years ago, we were evicted from Sollas, a fertile part in the north of the island. There we lived in ease and plenty, in a happy and prosperous condition. Then we realised that might was right. First we were deprived of a large portion of our grazing and arable land, which was added to another farm; then we were evicted. In "The Battle of Sollas" (when police with batons tried to protect the evicting party against people throwing stones and trying to prevent them) one at least died, others were permanently disabled, and some imprisoned. Many were compelled to emigrate, fever broke out on the *Hercules* (the vessel which conveyed some to Australia) to which most of them succumbed. Some were buried in Ireland, and others committed to a watery grave.

'We, the remainder, were given labour by the Highland Committee to keep us alive, until we were finally sent to Locheport where we still struggle to exist. I remember the soldiers coming from Inverness. It was in autumn they were pulling down the houses. It was during the winter that the first houses were built at Locheport. We only built turf houses at first. The houses we have now were all built at our own expense. I believe, if I had another man putting mine into the very condition in which it is, it would have come to £13 or £14. We had to quarry the stones out of a hill.

All that remains of the Free Church where the Commission held its meeting at Locheport on 30th May, 1883.

'This was a wild, bleak, barren, mossy heath when we came here. We have laboured for the last thirty years and our crofts will not yield us enough food to support our families for two months of the year. The place is overcrowded, 34 crofts with 40 families on them where there used to be three. There is no fishing here and no kelp now. All who are able to leave at the beginning of summer to earn their livelihood as best they may by sea and land. We are poor and would like to move to where we can live by the produce of our labours in the soil.

One of the thatched houses people built for themselves at Locheport, beside the ruins of another.

'I had many relatives among those who were sent away to America. Several reached America but very few are alive today. We heard that some are well off and some are not. None of those who were evicted ever came back'.

Houses, outhouses, potatoes protected by a dyke, and free ranging cattle at Carinish, North Uist in 1910.

Sollas looking towards Middlequarter.

John MacDonald's house and farm of Newton in 1872 and proof that he at least was growing turnips.

The estate of North Uist was sold by Lord MacDonald to Sir John Campbell Orde in 1855. John MacDonald, the farmer of Newton, acted as factor and, exceptionally for a factor, he was actually praised by other witnesses. He gave a good account of the changes in farming practice he had seen:

'People were more comfortably off before the potato disease than they are now. They had more mutton, more milk, but less tea. They were less finely clothed but they were comfortably clothed in clothes of their own making.

'Now they can send their produce away to market. They could not send their sheep away in those days. There was no steam navigation. Now all the crofters have sheep of the black-faced breed. They keep the ewe lambs and they sell their *wedder* (male) lambs and their *slack ewes* (which have missed producing a lamb), principally to Glasgow. Most of their *hoggs* (young sheep) are wintered in the houses. Turnips would be an advantage to them if they grew a few (but an earlier witness said they didn't grow turnips in case foolish boys stole them).

'I remember when there was no meal sold except the produce of the country but now they require to buy food from the south. In a great measure, I think it is due to the change in the seasons — the winter or spring weather goes so far into summer. Grain is principally grown to provide fodder for cattle and horses, and they keep more cattle now. The price of cattle now is very much above what it was in former times, and it pays better to raise cattle and with the produce of those cattle to buy meal in the south. That is the general practice in the island. Also since these clearances took place, there could not be as much land over the whole of North Uist turned over by the plough as there was fifty years ago. I cannot say in acres how much land was thrown out of cultivation but there is a great deal.

'The crofters all require two horses. They have a long way to carry seaweed, and in spring they plough with a pair of ponies. If a crofter paying £5 rent keeps two mares, he must sell a colt every year. I've seen a year-old fetch £17 but at the present time a good average would be £7– £8. The old Highland ponies are dying out fast. The last I got was a Welsh pony which I took from the Duke of Sutherland. Also a crofter with four cows ought to be able to sell two *stirks* (young bullocks) every year. Some have four stirks, others none in a year. Their value is generally from £5 to £6 each.'

People of the Long Island
Lewis and Harris

Lewis

Leaving North Uist, the Commission held a meeting at Obbe, later to become Lord Leverhulme's ambitious fishing centre in Harris and called Leverburgh, and then made their surprise visit to St Kilda (page 76). Then they made stops on the west coast of Lewis to hear from the crofters on the Matheson estate. James Matheson was a partner in Jardine, Matheson and Co., one of the leading firms involved in opening up trade with China through Hong Kong, sending in opium from India and bringing out tea. He returned home with a fortune in his mid-forties and paid £190,000 for the estate of Lewis in 1844. Since then the population had increased by 50% in forty years, from 17,000 in 1841 to 25,800 in 1881. While the Commissioners were busy in the west, the town of Stornoway in the east was the scene of a remarkable demonstration by the recently formed Lewis Land Law Reform Association. Many fishermen gave up a day's fishing on 1st June to be there, and some walked thirty or forty miles to get there. Reports differ on the number present: 2,000 according to *The Scotsman*, about 4,000 according to Alexander Morrison 'Big Alick', president of the Stornoway branch, but they marched from Bayhead through the streets out to the market stance at Marybank, with pipes playing and banners aloft bearing slogans such as 'Land to the People'. The Stornoway branch officials encouraged delegates for crofting townships in Lewis to put their grievances in writing and to speak out without fear when they faced the Royal Commission.

Barvas

The *Lively* could not always land the Commissioners close to their next place of meeting, due to the lack of harbours on the west coast. To get to Barvas on 6th June, they had to drive twelve miles along the coast road from Carloway Loch. They saw many townships on the way and watched a man grinding *bere* (a hardier coarser kind of barley) in a simple water-mill, before entering the Free Church for their meeting at 11 o'clock.

John Matheson, a 68-year-old crofter, told them about life in Upper Barvas where there were twenty-four crofts, compared with twelve fifty years ago, the result of the natural increase of the place:

'My rent is £3,6s., not including taxes, 5s. for road money and 1s. for *hen money*. Yes, I remember a factor called Knox (John Knox, the factor when the estate belonged to MacKenzie of Seaforth) very well indeed. Everybody would know him. There was nobody in the whole island like him — he was a great big, fat man. I remember hens being delivered in his time (to the castle, instead of hen money) and I remember him exacting a week's work from the people, and failing that, 5s. instead.

'I have too many animals for my croft this year, more than the croft can properly feed. I have no summing: that has gone out of fashion. We always buy more or less fodder for our stock in winter, but we get a good deal of their provender out of the shore — sea-ware. The sheep don't eat sea-ware, but the cattle and the horses do. They go away down to the sea themselves to eat it. Of course, the people bring it up for them too. It is very good for cows in the way of making milk, especially at this time of the year, and straw is the best food to go along with it.

Milking a cow up at the Barvas shielings.

'The people are not so well off now as fifty years ago. They cannot be, with the number of people here. I remember that fifty years ago we were clothed with the wool and the homemade cloth of our district. Today they have senseless rags that they buy here and there in other places. Yes, I know that the people all around you are well-dressed and decently dressed, but they are all in their best today!

'Their houses are considerably better now. I have myself built a poor house in many ways (I've built two in my time) but it is superior to the house my father had.

'I quite approve of there being no public houses or places for the sale of liquor in the country except in Stornoway. There was such a day when I used to frequent them but even I gave it up entirely. I don't know if there are many temperance people now. I never took the pledge myself.

'My family is now very small, they are scattered here and there but when they were together I would consider £20 a very moderate allowance for what I had to purchase to feed them. Milk and butter are scarce now, and we give children tea now to make up for the loss of milk. I was the father of a family before I could distinguish between tea and coffee. Children now can tell the difference before they are four years of age. They are not so innocent as I was.

'People here still go to the shielings (summer pastures in the hills) regularly. Probably there will be two heads of cattle on the average going to the summer pasture from each house, and a female always accompanies them. Sometimes two neighbours entrust the care of their cattle to one person. They send them about this time and keep them there about six weeks. The women stay all that time in the shielings (and sleep in little huts). Yes, I have heard something about people going in a sort of procession singing a sort of chant when they went to the shielings but I cannot give any opinion about it. I believe it must have been long ago. What I heard was that they used to sing, but it was not the Psalms of David, whatever.

'Yes, I have seen vessels of clay being made by the people of Barvas. They made all sorts. We have them yet; there is one person here who makes them yet. She can't make jars with narrow necks but she would make crocks for butter. Some of this woman's work was sent to Edinburgh (probably to the National Museum of Antiquities' collection), and gentlemen who came to the place used to hunt her up and get some of the work she did. In the days of my grandfather and great-grandfather, these clay vessels were in most common use. I believe this art was of native growth'.

Typical Barvas pottery.

John Matheson agreed to sell a piece of pottery, a butter dish from his grandfather's time to Lord Napier, who stayed on that evening with Mr Fraser MacKintosh to examine other old pots made from the coarse clay of Barvas.

Lionel, Ness

The next meeting in the school at Lionel was the most northerly in their tour of the Long Island. But in ten days time, the *Lively* would be carrying them much farther north, for meetings in Shetland. They were struck by the physique and smartness of the Ness fishermen in their blue trousers and jerseys, and by the greater number of crofters than usual who had some other skilled occupation, besides their crofts. Murdo MacKay from Lionel, for example, was a weaver, when there were still very few weavers in Lewis, and Donald MacIver of Cross of Ness was a blacksmith who told them there was another blacksmith at Swainbost not far away. Most of the local men were ling fishermen and the Commissioners had the chance to see for themselves the little harbour which was being constructed at that time to shelter their boats at Port of Ness. A pier was being run along the top of the rocks and boulders and the harbour being excavated to over thirteen feet, but it was to be a tidal harbour, too small for the herring boats from the north-east. They heard from John MacLeod, the boat-builder, about the boats he built and the local fishing:

'I'm just a boat-builder, and supply fishermen with boats, six or seven a year. I build for the fishermen and the curers, but more for the curers. Usually, the curers give the crews the boats on three years' shares. The boat comes to £30, and that is £10 a year for three seasons. If the crew can clear it off in three seasons, the boat is theirs.

'The shell of the boat, like the ones you saw on the shore here, and the ropes and the mast, cost only £30. The sail costs £8, but the boat cannot go fishing without lines. The total cost is about £42 or £43.

'The line fisherman's way of working is to go out and set their lines, and they have a big stone at the end of the lines and a rope up to the top of the water with a buoy. When the Stornoway herring boats come, they are setting their own nets and these are drifted, and they carry away the lines. It is a very good boat that takes 1,000 ling this year. I remember when they were taking 6,000.

'My suggestion is that a larger harbour should be built here and they should get large boats as their neighbours do from the east coast. Now all these men have to go to the east coast, and be under masters who can do with them as they like, and they (the local men) have not even one net of their own. I have seen them coming home with from £5 to £20; and some with less than £5 some years'.

The successors of John MacLeod at Port of Ness still building the same kind of boat.

Last day on the *Lively*

That evening, 7th June, the *Lively* sailed round the Butt of Lewis and headed for Stornoway at a good pace. For the last few weeks the ship had become a floating home for the members of the Royal Commission and their staff. Robert Holden, the clerk, whose last job had been in a very different environment in London, and Irvine Smith the shorthand writer messed in the wardroom, while the Commissioners and the Secretary dined with the captain, Commander Parr, in the saloon at a cost to the Treasury for food and wine of 15s. a day. Living at sea kept them free from the risk of pressure being exerted on them, either by landlords and factors on the one hand or crofters on the other. Unlike them, the *Scotsman* correspondent who travelled all over the island in the coach belonging to William MacKay, the chamberlain of the Matheson estate and was entertained as the personal guest of his chief accountant, was considered to be acting as the mouthpiece of the chamberlain. If there were domestic difficulties in living aboard the *Lively*, they were minor ones, such as the Commissioners' washing, which they had to pay for themselves 'at somewhat exorbitant rates' for having it done at Oban and transported there and back to wherever their next port of call might be.

Such thoughts were far from their minds that sunny evening, however, after a long day's meeting and the prospect of difficult meetings in Stornoway to come. Lord Napier, suffering somewhat from sea-sickness, had just received news that his mother had died, and had been lying down. As the captain and the Commissioners chatted after dinner, the off-duty sailors were on the fore-deck having a sing-song as usual. The *Lively* was doing 10½ knots with the pilot, John MacDonald, on the quarter-deck in charge. The navigating officer, Lieut. A. S. Mills, had left him unknown to the captain, and gone for his dinner down below, when suddenly the whole ship shook, there was a rasping crash as a jagged rock pierced her bottom and the ship came to a dead stop. She was stuck on a well-known, but unmarked hazard, the Chicken Rock and was shipping water fast.

The Lively *wrecked on the Chicken Rock, 7th June, 1883.*

There was time for most of the passengers and crew to pack their belongings as Captain Campbell of the *Mary Ann* of Glasgow, a steamer on her way to Oban with a cargo of herring, turned his ship round and came to their aid. *Lively*'s boats were lowered and Sheriff Nicolson, the Secretary and clerk distinguished themselves by saving most of the Royal Commission's papers first. The Commissioners, their staff and the newspaper reporters who were with them reached Stornoway on board the *Mary Ann* at one o'clock in the morning and all 78 members of the crew were also taken off safely. When the tide went out, the stern of the *Lively* sank and left her bow high out of the water. Her back appeared to be broken. It was a sad end for a smart and fast ship, a 1000-ton wooden steam yacht built in 1870, which had had 250 h.p. engines and paddle wheels, as well as sails.

The Commissioners personally had all had a narrow escape but several of their party, Lochiel, Malcolm MacNeill and Robert Holden, lost their baggage and all their clothes. Although their papers were in some disarray, they too were safe. They sent a message to tell their printer to print more forms but how were they to carry on their enquiry when their means of transport was breaking up out there on the Chicken Rock? They would hold the meetings they had arranged in Stornoway, it was decided; HMS *Jackal*, which had come north to see if the *Lively* could be saved, would take them south to Tarbert to finish their work in Harris; and their meetings in the Northern Isles were postponed until some other ship could take them there.

As for the *Lively*, valuable equipment was stripped out but all the efforts to pull her off the rocks failed. She broke up in a gale on 27th June (just before the closing date for tenders for her as scrap) and people were finding tables, doors, masts and bits of the deck swept up on beaches and rocks, but the forepart was successfully floated and towed into Stornoway by the *Lochiel*.

But how had it been possible for such an accident to happen? The Court-Martial at Devonport on 28th June blamed it on an error of judgement by the pilot, in spite of the tributes the *Lively*'s officers paid to his skill. One influence on the ship's speed at the time had been the captain's desire to reach Stornoway harbour as early as possible because of the number of fishing boats also wanting to berth in it. The ship's position before the crash probably resulted from the discovery by the pilot of Lord Napier's condition, which led him to alter course and make for smoother waters. Then in the slanting evening sun it seems he could not see the shore and did not realise he was in so close. The Court-Martial made two startling discoveries: that the naval officers had not been making normal navigating checks on the ship's course when they had a pilot who, they thought, 'knew the way', and secondly that, although Captain MacDonald had taken vessels into Stornoway twenty or thirty times before, this was the first time he had come in from the north. Commander Parr and Lieut. Mills were 'severely reprimanded and dismissed their ship' — justified probably, but a bit late considering where their ship now was!

Stornoway

Aware of the demonstration in Stornoway the previous week, the Commissioners expected they would hear more extreme views on the land question from witnesses, and they did. Donald Martin from Back, for example, told them he feared there was a danger that the younger men might rise 'as the clans of old rose, if they do not get a hold over the land of which they were deprived for the sake of sheep, deer and grouse'. Alexander Morrison of the Land Law Reform League maintained that if all the land in Lewis, sheep farms, deer forests and croft land were shared equally by all the people, Lewis could keep in a contented way 70,000 people, nearly three times as many as there were in 1883. On the other side, the chamberlain of the Matheson estate, William MacKay, declared that the crofters were not oppressed. Their rents, for example, had not been increased for thirty years and Sir James Matheson had spent over quarter of a million pounds on improvements on the island of Lewis, building schools and roads and providing the first steamer, the *Mary Jane*, to connect Lewis with the mainland. He also built a chemical works and a brickworks, and supplied meal and seed to crofters in years of famine. William MacKay insisted that £100,000 had been expended on improving land on the estate but when questioned closely on this, he had to admit that only £1,500 of it had been on land in new townships for crofters to move to, which made the claim the Commission had heard from the Branahine crofters that not 'one single shilling was spent on improving our crofts or houses' appear to be substantially correct.

William MacKay had been in the estate office of the Matheson estate practically all his life. When asked if he had Gaelic himself, he replied, 'A sort of it'. When the Royal Commission was set up, he took fright at what they might ask and what they might find out. He raised difficulties about simple questions in the written Return that all factors had to make — the crofter's name, the area of arable land or the number of animals he had.

Croft-houses near Stornoway in 1900 — note the roped roofs, chimneys and peat stacks.

Telling him to consult the estate books or ask the crofters was no help. The estate did not know and in his desperation he declared that you could not expect a crofter to have any idea whatever of the extent of an acre of land. Lady Matheson, in charge of the estate after her husband died in 1878, refused to pay for extra staff to complete the forms: then, when it looked as if the Government would make some payment (later discovered to be never more than 3d per croft) he took on two surveyors at £100 a year each and would have employed more if he could. When these strange surveyors from the estate office suddenly appeared with their chains to measure croft land, however, they only aroused the suspicions of the crofters, who sometimes chased them away. The contribution the Government paid the estate in the end for details about 2948 crofters was only £36,15s.3d.

Difficult to hear when giving evidence and with a liking for long statements containing extracts from the Old Statistical Account in the 1790s while admitting he had not read the New Statistical Account published fifty years later, William MacKay was not a persuasive witness. Neither was his opponent, Alexander Morrison, the young leader of the Land Law Reform Association. He was high on emotive terms like 'oppression and slavery' and 'fixity of tenure' but low on factual knowledge of the island, which became evident when he was subjected to the kind of probing questions which the Commission usually reserved for factors.

That the Lewis crofters were poor and had too little land was obvious to the Commissioners: whether more of the people could make a living from the sea they discussed with Donald Smith, a fish-curer in Stornoway who had about eighty crews fishing for him. If more harbours and piers were built, there was scope in Lewis, he thought, for 180 more big boats, costing about £160 for each boat and its gear. Fish-curers like himself bought them and advanced them to crews, who paid them up at so much per year. As a curer, he also supplied fishermen in advance with meal and groceries and lines and hooks, and in return, the men sold their fish to him, usually at a price fixed before the season started. Did this mean that many of the boats and the families of the fishermen were in debt to the curers? Donald Smith said frankly that they were: 'The last three seasons have been rather backward, and there were very few of the boats clear'.

Harris

The loss of the *Lively* caused nationwide interest and the London *Graphic*'s artist suddenly found himself in Stornoway drawing the wreck. When the Royal Commission moved on in the *Jackal* to Tarbert in Harris, he was there, making interesting drawings of the place of meeting, the Free Church in Tarbert, and the people who were present. *The Graphic*, a weekly, cost its readers 6d., compared with 1d. for the daily *Scotsman*, and the text accompanying the drawings was intended to allow them a little laugh, with statements like this: 'In the Hebrides a barber would die of starvation; wild unkempt heads of hair are the fashion'. He should see us now!

One of the men he drew was old John MacDiarmid of Scalpay (page 78), and he described Lachlan Campbell of Scadabay with his strong features and iron-grey hair rising four inches above his forehead as 'looking like a Viking with a look of power in a face rarely seen'. Lachlan was a forty-three-year-old crofter who brought the Commissioners back to the basic condition of so many crofters, crowded into a small space. In his township where there were six families once, there were now eighteen:

'The families increased, and they must needs marry, and they married. When a man married he required to get a house, and there was no place for him to build it except on his father's lot. The eighteen are making their living in the place — each of them has a bit of the land that there is, and taking a living out of it, but they are all now in the same impoverished condition.

'I know that nobles and gentlemen have to send away their sons wherever they can make a living but they send them away with plenty of money to get homes and lands and sometimes well-paid jobs, when they become gentlemen. We poor people, sending our family away without perhaps as much money as will pay their passage, with insufficient clothing, and no education, often fear they will fare badly. They must buy clothes with the first wages they earn, and the first £1 they can spare must be sent home to keep their father and mother alive.

'Where there is only one son, he must needs remain at home to till the ground, but if there are several sons, why should the rest go away and be content to be bachelors for a time? A bachelor is an object of charity the world over. It is the first duty of a man — especially a Harris man — to get married and increase the number of inhabitants, and to get land to occupy it. What is written is that "He gave the land to the children of men".'

Lachlan had summed up the crofter's predicament but as long as much of North Harris was deer forest and South Harris under sheep, the crofters had too little of the land. They might look to the sea, as John McDiarmid's neighbours in Scalpay did, or else to the women of Harris to supplement their income. The women were proverbial, another witness said, 'for their good spinning, their good weaving and their good making of clothes' (as pages 85–89 show) and thanks to the efforts of the Dowager Countess of Dunmore in finding markets for the webs of cloth they wove, 'you hear of Harris tweeds, here, there and everywhere'.

'Looking like a Viking', almost certainly Lachlan Campbell of Scudabay.

An older witness, probably John MacDiarmid.

Faces in the crowd at Tarbert.

Shetland Fishermen

When the Commissioners resumed their islands tour in July, it was not on a Royal Naval vessel. The Admiralty declared they had no suitable vessel available — but they may have been unwilling to risk losing another — and suggested hiring the *North Star*, a 400-ton steamer from Messrs. James Currie and Co., of Leith. The cost, £1500 for six weeks with the Government paying for messing, coals, pilotage and port charges, almost caused the Home Office to take fright but there was no alternative and the ship was engaged.

Commanded by Captain Ritchie, the *North Star* called at Kirkwall to make final arrangements for the meetings in Orkney on their return from Shetland. They knew the people they would meet in the Northern Isles would be different, in speech for example and their land law, due to Viking influence and settlement going back to about the year 800. Abandoning the idea of landing on Fair Isle because of the heavy swell, they arrived in Shetland at the height of the fishing season and on their first day in Lerwick Court House found only two witnesses ready to give evidence, a fish-curer and a crofter-fisherman.

Arthur James Hay, the fish-curer

In business for 25 years or more as a merchant and fish-curer, he explained how his own firm supplied the fishermen with big boats adapted for the herring fishing:

'The boats are 43 feet to 50 feet of keel, 14 feet beam. They are wholly decked boats now, weighing 20 to 25 tons. The boats are not hired to the men; they are provided to the men and they endeavour to pay them off, out of their earnings. There are generally six men in a boat, and the half of their earnings go in towards the price of a boat. Many of the boats you see here are the property of the men who work them. The price of the fish is fixed in advance, usually before they commence, in the winter season and we settle with them in October or November'.

Later Sheriff Charles Rampini explained the difficulties many fishing families got into through having goods advanced to them by the curers before and during the fishing season and being shocked to discover, not having kept accounts, that their earnings from the fish they caught were not enough to wipe out their debt. He thought the old method of dealing between merchant and fisherman was pernicious as it prevented the fisherman's standard of living from rising. Worse, after the fishing tragedy of 20th July, 1881 when 63 fishermen perished, 36 of them from one fishing station, Gloup in North Yell, who left behind 24 widows and 56 children of school age or younger, he discovered as chairman of the Shetland Fishermen's Widows' Relief Fund that most of the men who lost their lives were in debt. His committee refused to take responsibility either for their debts or for the loss of the boats in which they had been fishing.

Donald Moar of North Yell, fisherman

This young fisherman took a day off from the fishing to appear before the Commissioners in the Reading Room of Baltasound in Unst. He came from Cullivoe in the north-east of North Yell, not far from Gloup which had suffered such losses of life at sea two years before. Donald was 23, one of a crew of seven in a boat they had from William Paul, a curer, on the *half-catch* system:

'He owns the boat and we give him the fish, and we get half the fish for our trouble. He keeps the boat in working order and gets half the fish. We're at the herring fishing now, at Uyea Sound off Unst and we also fish at the west side of the island. We'll be at the herring fishing till September. We were at the cod and ling fishing from the month of March and gave it up on 12th June.

'We just work at the land through the winter and repair the fishing material, and when the weather is good enough to enable us to go off to the fishing, we go in four-oared boats round the shore. We get cod there principally, not in large quantities, about 1 or 1½ cwt. in a day.

'We have dealt with the curer this while back: but now that Scotch curers are coming into the place and giving good prices for fish, they are getting their eyes opened. The Scotch curers bring supplies too. If you have no money, your curer has to supply you. We settle with him when the fishing is done — about Martinmas (11th November). For catching herring we have from the start of the season 150 crans at 15s. to 1st August; and then we get £1 a cran for 250 crans; and for any beyond that quantity 14s. if we get that many. The fish after the 1st August are more valuable — they are full, they are considered to be in their prime and cure better. We expect a good fishing this year: there are plenty of fish about. 300 crans is considered a very good fishing in the season, but sometimes we make more than that. We have got 100 crans already this season.

As an artist Frank Barnard freely shows two fishing seasons in one picture, herring gutting and packing on the left, and drying white fish on the right, 1890.

'We get 7s.6d. for cod, 8s.6d. for ling, 5s. for *tusk* per cwt. (torsk, of the cod family) and 10s. for halibut up to the 6th May. They ice halibut and send them to Birmingham, Leeds and London (the Commission had heard of halibut being used as bait at Ness in Lewis, because it was too far away from a market). The bait we use for the long line deep sea fishing is herring. We catch them all the year round for bait. When you don't catch herring you don't set lines. The small boats use mussel bait but the large boats don't. We just give the fish to the curer. We have nothing to do but take off the heads. We get the heads and liver and keep them for our own purposes. We take nothing to do with cleaning or drying.

'When we settle with the curer, we get the balance in money the night we settle. The fishermen are getting better on now; the big boats get more money. Twenty years ago, Shetland was very poor but now more and more the fishermen are clear at settling time.

'Oh yes, I'd prefer to have a boat of my own. I could go to any curer I liked and get bounty too. They give better prices to a man who has a boat of his own but there is only one crew in this place who have been able to get a boat of their own. A big boat is much better than the old *sixern* (a six-oared Shetland fishing boat), not so much loss of life in them. The small boats were just skiffs: a big boat would live where a small boat would not'.

Fishermen's huts for the season at Stenness west of Hillswick, Shetland.

Walter Sutherland of Nesting, formerly a fisherman

'Yes, Scotch curers have done much good to Shetland — they have raised men's wages. When I had a boat in Lerwick, I had never above 1s. for taking charge. There were four men besides me. We got 4s.8d. for the cran of herring. I got 1s. and the other men in the boat got 10d. Now they get 20s. amongst them'.

When it was put to him that he was speaking about Scotsmen as if he belonged to another country, Walter replied, 'This is a Scottish island, but it is those who have come from the mainland of Scotland who have done good to Shetland. If they hadn't come, fishermen would be receiving now the same wages as when I was a lad'.

The herring boom which drew them up to Shetland had happened recently and suddenly. Figures the sheriff supplied to the Royal Commission showed that the number of people employed had gone up from less than 1000 in 1878 to over 4,300 in 1882, and the number of barrels of cured herring shipped out had increased from 8,500 to 134,000 in the same period. At the end of July 1883, *The Scotsman* reckoned that at Baltasound where 11 boats had been operating the previous year, there were 200 this year, and 2000 people in felt-roofed wooden shanties to deal with the catch.

David Ogilvie, teacher, Mid Yell

Young lads had been employed as beach boys for many years in drying cod and ling but the herring boom suddenly made it almost impossible to get children to come to school at all:

'I have 71 on the school register but there are about thirty away just now rolling barrels. When they can work and make money at the herrings, they give no excuse for being absent. Only the other day a parent applied to have his girl's name taken off the roll. She is about twelve years of age and she's *gipping* (gutting) herring. This is a family of four men and two women. The women are gipping herring and the men are at the fishing. They have two girls under leaving age in the family and not content with six of the grown-up members earning wages, they've applied to get the elder girl off the roll. They think education is of no value in this part of the world — better to do a little work and get pennies for it'.

James Barclay and James R. Sutherland, ministers

Eighty years of age and still the minister of Mid Yell where he had been ordained in 1844, James Barclay welcomed the herring fishing for the opportunities of employment it brought to everyone, men and women, boys and girls. Many of the gutters came from Peterhead, Aberdeen, Inverness, and as far away as Argyll. Wooden houses heated with stoves were put up quickly to house them. 'This is the first time we've had these strangers', he said, 'and they appear quiet, decent people, decently dressed, and some of them come to church'.

James R. Sutherland of Northmavine, another minister with long service in his parish agreed, having found that the women who came were lodged 'in a very comfortable nice place' on Hillswick Bay. Not many of the women of his parish were working at the herring; they were too busy in the hosiery trade. The recent loss of the common grazing for Shetland sheep, however, made a teacher express the fear that their young women would be forced out of knitting beautiful fine hosiery and left with no option but the disagreeable and degrading occupation of gutting fish.

Packing herrings and loading at Holmsgarth near Lerwick in the mid-1880s.

Fishermen and the land

Would the Shetland herring boom last? The doubts in everyone's mind were voiced by John Spence, the teacher at Nesting. He knew that catches of cod and ling were low in winter and prices no more than ¾d. a pound:

'The fisherman needs a croft to fall back on, its harvest (more potatoes than grain as a rule) to sustain him, and his home to shelter him. Potatoes and fish are the staple food of Shetland'.

Donald Moar also felt that his croft was important. His family ran it when he was away and he worked it in winter. He had 3 cows and 6 ponies but no sheep, and he had to pay someone else to get grazing for the ponies. Like nearly all the small farmers in Shetland, he had lost his right to the *scathold* (the common grazing). In his case, it was John Walker, the factor, who took it away. The Commissioners were to hear the same complaint again and again in Shetland: except for the difference in name, they might have been back in Skye hearing Angus Stewart deploring the loss of Ben Lee.

The typical Shetland township, the sheriff explained to them at Lerwick, was a collection of stone cottages surrounded by *feul* (turf) dykes, separating the arable land inside from the scathold beyond it. Each owner of arable was entitled to a share of the scathold, so named because it paid *scat* (land tax) to the Crown. He believed that the bigger feudal landlords who had acquired land more recently had no right to it. John Spence, the teacher, expressed the view most people held in Shetland, however, when he said:

'The crofters have possessed the rights of pasturage on the hills during a period of at least 900 years'.

Thomas Henderson of Olnafirth, Delting defined how extensive the right was, 'in days of old, from the highest clod of the hill to the lowest stone on the beach, the tenants are entitled to the pasture when they took a farm'. The dues they used to pay for it separately had been gradually incorporated into their rents, and when the rents increased, so did the amount they were paying for the common pasture.

One of the crofters on Whalsay, William Hutcheson, described how the division of the scathold had affected his island and himself:

'It was taken off us for the sheep farm on the island. Half of the island was taken off for that, and so 100 families are left on the other half of the island, with half the scathold. The other half goes to this one man, Zachary MacAulay Hamilton, the son of the minister of Bressay, who has the farm. Now I have no place to tether a cow in, and cannot have a drop of milk'.

Loss of scathold affected other crofters seriously too. Unable to keep Shetland sheep, they lacked fine wool for hosiery and cloth-making and took to wearing cotton. Without grazing, Shetland cattle didn't know where the hill was any more and had to be housed in byres all night from October until May. There they had so little to eat, according to Alexander Walker in Mid Yell, that in the spring they could not get up by themselves and had to be lifted to their feet. Some families without a milk supply turned to buying syrup for their children. Not everyone could keep Shetland ponies. Gentlemen who had enough pasture could keep the breed small through careful selection and get high prices for their ponies, and there was also a good demand for them in the south as pit ponies, but many of the crofters were left with none. They could not plough and had to delve with the spade, and carry everything on their backs because they had no carts. Much of this kind of work fell on the women: as Walter Williamson of West Burra put it, 'The poor women work a good deal harder than many of the rich men's horses'.

Paying the rent

With his earnings from fishing, Donald Moar had less difficulty than most in paying the rent of his croft, but Lawrence Jamieson of South Cunningsburgh, the first Shetland fisherman to appear at Lerwick, had a grievance about rent which he thought had gone on too long. He had to do three days work a year for every *merk* of land (usually about two acres) he held and also give a fowl to the proprietor. The work was general work on the proprietor's farm, where he would be given two meals, breakfast and dinner, but no wages, and if he failed to turn up for work, he would be charged 2s. for each day he missed. Old John Bruce of Sumburgh as proprietor maintained that he needed such labour to cut his peats and bring them in, hoe his potatoes and make his hay during the busy time in summer. His son who now ran the estate declared that Lawrence Jamieson was exaggerating. The labour dues were three days per farm, not per merk; they were supposed to be the rent for the crofter's house and his right to cut peats; and as for the historic practice of bringing a fowl as part of the rent, Lawrence Jamieson hadn't brought one since 1880!

In a community like Fetlar where only a few men were fishermen, the minister said it was the custom to sell a pony to make up the rent. A one-year old would often bring in £4–£5, a two-year old £9 and a three-year old might be worth as much as £12. Old people, like Erasmus Doull of North Roe in Northmavine who still had enough pasture, got money from selling one or two cattle a year and, he said, perhaps twenty pounds of butter at 10d. to 1s. a pound.

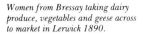

Women from Bressay taking dairy produce, vegetables and geese across to market in Lerwick 1890.

Being self-sufficient

Erasmus would not sell the wool from his sheep, however. It was spun in his house, woven by a local weaver and made into a suit for him by a tailor eight miles away. He grew enough corn to keep his family and animals about half the year. Besides oats, he grew potatoes, a few turnips and a little bere. He ground a little grain at home and the rest he put out to the mill, but not a local mill. He couldn't get any milled now if the steamer didn't bring it, but he remembered little mills grinding in valleys in the hills where, he said, 'the water came down and heaved it round'.

A merchant at Ollaberry, not far from him, found crofting families liked to buy some wheaten flour to balance up the oatmeal from their own grain for making their scones and bread. He thought it was good for them to make their own. 'I could sell a good deal more baker's bread, but I don't want to do that', he said, 'I think it would encourage laziness'.

Rooin', plucking the wool by hand from Shetland sheep. This was taken in Foula in 1933.

On sea and overseas

Many Shetland men still gained a living from the sea in other ways. D. C. Edmonston, lessee and factor of the estate of Buness, told them whaling ships from Peterhead and Dundee still came to Lerwick to pick up crews. An agent in Lerwick engaged them, arranging terms with the captain, generally so much in advance, a stated wage by the month and so much oil money. Some, like Hugh Hughson of Gossabrough in East Yell, joined the merchant navy. He was 37 now, he said, he'd gone to sea when he was 16 and had sailed to India, China and the colonies and had met a great many Shetlanders on ships abroad. When his brother died, Hugh stayed home to help to bring up his brother's family of eight children, but he believed he could make a better living in another country. He liked to keep informed about the outside world and read *The Scotsman* or *The Liverpool Mercury*.

Many Shetlanders had gone to Australia and New Zealand in recent years. John Omand of Mid Yell declared that, of all the places abroad where he had met other Shetland people, the one which attracted him most was Victoria where many of them were digging for gold. In 1874–75, emigration agents had stumped round Shetland and persuaded a great many people through assisted passages to go out to New Zealand.

'The people went of their own free will', James Robertson of Happy Hansel in the parish of Walls recalled. 'There was no money required; the emigration was free. When they got abroad, they just worked at the best thing that turned up. Whole families went, men, women and children. It was the New Zealand Government that took them out and supplied them with food, but the families had to find their own way to London'.

Their departure, he believed, brought one benefit to their neighbours in Shetland. By reducing the number wanting crofts it kept rents low.

Orkney Farmers

At first, few people in Orkney made much effort to be ready for the arrival of the Royal Commission. The exception was on the island of Sanday, where several meetings were held, all reported in the national press. For the third meeting on 18th June, forty people gathered in Edwin Sinclair the tailor's barn and William Muir of Templehall, a small farmer and merchant who acted as chairman, was appointed to be their delegate, and it was agreed to send a letter summarising their grievances to the Commission in Edinburgh. Elsewhere, the South Ronaldsay men were too busy at the fishing; in Harray on the Mainland complaining of having too little notice of a meeting, people had no delegates appointed; and no one appeared before the Commission on Sanday to represent North Ronaldsay, whose delegate, Mr Grant the Free Church minister, was reported to be on his way to New Zealand! Was it, as William Muir suggested, that people were afraid they might offend the proprietor? When Sheriff Nicolson reminded him that in the whole of the Western

Sanday landscape at harvest time.

Isles, the Commission had encountered no lack of evidence and no lack of freedom of speech, whatever the proprietors might think or do, Muir replied that Orkney people were more retiring, and perhaps more timid. But perhaps they really did have fewer grievances. The speed with which the Royal Commission collected its evidence in Orkney — in three days compared with fifteen in Skye — could be construed to support either view until the facts they discovered are examined, but their encounter in Kirkwall Sheriff Court with the owner of the island of Rousay, General Burroughs, left them in no doubt that there was at least one frightening landlord in Orkney.

The crofter-mason and the landlord

Almost at the last minute, on Saturday 14th July, crofters from all over Rousay had met in the Mill of Banks in very large numbers. Their landlord, the General, was away at the time on holiday in Germany. They complained of big rises in their rents as a result of improvements on their holdings which they had made themselves, and they appointed delegates, one of them James Leonard, a crofter and mason, to speak for them.

Appearing before the Commission, James Leonard asked for the customary assurance from the landlord that they would not suffer injury for the evidence they were about to give. Lieut-General Frederick William Traill Burroughs, an incomer to Orkney who had served in the Crimea and the Indian Mutiny, would not give it.

'It is contrary to human nature', he said, 'to be so friendly disposed to them as to others who do not make complaints. My intention would be for them to go away simply. They are not slaves: they are free men and need not remain here if they don't like'.

It made no difference when Lord Napier explained that they were sitting as a Royal Commission with the object and duty of eliciting the truth. The General replied with questions:

'Is the property mine or is it not mine? If it is mine, surely I can do what I consider best for it? My intention is to try and make the people labourers and throw their holdings into larger farms, but not to remove them from their houses'.

Having received no assurance, James Leonard decided to go ahead anyway, happy that the Commissioners had had this opportunity to experience the attitude of the landlord for themselves. Where he lived at Digro, the first house was built by his father on the *commonty* and their croft of eight acres was won by his father out of the heathery hillside. His father paid no rent at all until the General came: the rent he put on was low at first, only £1.2s., but it had gone up and up to £4 as a tenant-at-will. When his father died last year, James stayed on in the croft where, being a mason, he had built a good house for his family of nine children. He knew he had no security and no claim for compensation should he ever be evicted. He cultivated about three of their poor acres and kept a cow. He didn't get constant work as a mason and one summer he'd gone to Glasgow to work. On the island, he'd been paid 1s.6d. a day, but 3s. was the general thing.

As an example of the terror the landlord caused on Rousay, he told the story of an old woman who had a croft and was on her death-bed.

'The proprietor visited her and told her she would have to leave it, because he was going to give it to another person. She said she would never leave it until she was put to a house from which no man could remove her. He said, "What house is that?" and she said, "Where I shall be buried"; and he struck his stick on the ground and said, "Would you like to be buried under this floor?" ' The minister agreed that the story was true, having heard it from the woman and her daughter.

When asked about it, General Burroughs insisted, 'I can say nothing, I don't remember any such thing', yet he was the only person to name her as 'Mrs Cooper on her deathbed'. Even then he did not think of expressing any regret, until he was prompted by Lord Napier, that he might have said something like it or given the wrong impression. He was amazed to discover the spirit of opposition delegates had expressed against him and would be glad to be rid of them. 'I want a contented people round me', he affirmed.

He talked of the improvements he had made on the big farms and to benefit the whole island — roads, regular steamers, mail daily, 'and a runner round the island'. He scoffed at the old idea of the commonty belonging to the people. It belonged to the various proprietors and had been divided between them. 'The people have as much right to my common as I have to their clothes. The land is mine and their hats and coats are theirs'.

James Leonard's statement of his charges as a mason astonished the General. 'He has always charged me 4s. a day for any masonwork he's done for me', he maintained. 'He is also precentor in a church (the Free Church) and he's always well paid for what he does. I know he has a large family, but they are growing up: some are herds and some are this and that. When I see him and his family at church, they are always dressed in the latest fashion'.

Given the chance to reply, James Leonard said if his family were well-dressed, it was they, and not he, who paid for it out of their wages; and his young children were certainly not dressed in Paris fashions, in fact, they weren't properly dressed at all.

Not long after leaving Orkney, the Royal Commission was to hear from General Burroughs again, when he forwarded a copy of an unsigned letter he had received which threatened him.

'If you remove one of them (the delegates who gave evidence) there shall be Blood Shed for if I meet you Night or day or any where that I get a Ball to Bare on you Curs your Blody head . . .'.

Burroughs suspected the letter was in a schoolboy's hand. In no time, he had two sheriffs and the superintendent of police crossing from Kirkwall to Rousay by fishery cruiser, and James Leonard's son Fred, aged 14, taken from the cattle he was tending. Without his father being informed, he was taken to the school and questioned and made to write phrases similar to those in the letter. Another boy aged 15 was taken off a fishing boat to Kirkwall and given the same treatment but none of the boys was charged. James Leonard was evicted, however, along with the delegate who supported him, James Grieve. The reason for their eviction — the evidence they had given to the Royal Commission — caused no small sensation in the national press.

A woman's case

The first woman to be questioned at any length by the Royal Commission was Mrs Georgina Inkster of Hammer, also on Rousay. Her husband, one of General Burrough's tenants, was said by the General to have assaulted the schoolteacher when he went to collect the school rates. Then the General took away their fifteen acres of land but left them in the house and proposed to make Hugh Inkster a labourer. Meanwhile Hugh had been away in Edinburgh in hospital and she was left destitute, trying to bring up a young family and keep his mother and sister as well, who were living in the end of her house. The inspector of poor would not grant them poor relief unless they went into the poor house, because the chairman of the parochial board, the General whose presence was necessary for any other decision to be made, was away in Germany on holiday at the time.

Bowmen wanting a croft

The Commission met Walter Traill Dennison in the fine U.P. Church on Sanday. He had the 300 acre farm of West Brough in the parish of Cross and was the author of *The Orcadian Sketchbook*, stories of local life written in the Orkney dialect. He explained that the married ploughmen on a farm who were in charge of a pair of horses lived in separate cottages, like hinds in the Lothians, but were called *bowmen*. Hill Burton derived the name from the old Scots word *boll*, a measure of meal (140 lbs), and a reminder of the days when they were paid in kind, not money. As late as 1851, he remembered them being paid only £7 and £7,10s. in money for the year but they also had a house rent free, two tons of coal and six bolls of meal a year, so much ground for planting their potatoes (60 chains as a rule) and a *Scotch pint* of milk a day (equal to three English pints).

In 1883, bowmen still received the same allowances in kind, while their
money wages had risen to £19,10s. Many of these men would have liked a
bit of land of their own when they were old where they could put their
farming experience to good use but, they complained, there was little
chance of them getting a croft on Sanday.

*A man and a woman carrying at the
peats on Hoy but with an ox-cart to
carry them home, 1889.*

Oncas and the farmer

W. T. Dennison explained to the Commissioners that the word *cottar* was
comparatively new in Orkney, where people like cottars were called *oncas*
because they were on call to work for the farmer. In return, the farmer
gave them a house, a bit of ground to cultivate called a *haerst* (harvest) *fee*,
and one or two *coogils* (bits of grazing for a cow).

James Cooper, a fisherman-cottar on Stronsay appeared with his father.
He complained that as cottars they were at the call of James Twatt, the
farmer, any time he wanted farming done at 2s. a day or draining at
2s.6d. a day, even when they might have the chance of earning far more
somewhere else.

Besides, they had to give food and lodging free to a woman working at
the farm all summer and autumn. She could well be a stranger coming to
live in their house and be fed at a cost, he said, of £3,10s. a year. During
the harvest, they had to send a man to work with her for five weeks for
£2,10s. wages, and they had to feed and pay a cook to prepare food for
them both and carry it out to the fields. James said they fished for cod,
herring and lobsters in summer, but what they wanted was 'to hold from
the proprietor and not be in bondage, and to have more ground'.

In reply, James Twatt contended that men's wages had been raised
although the women's had not, and that if cottars had women in their
own family, they usually sent them. He couldn't do without their labour as
a farmer. If they weren't bound to come, he would have to pay higher
wages to attract other people to work for him. Generally, he considered
whether it was convenient for a labourer to come.

'If a labourer comes to me and says, "I cannot come today, because it is
a good day for the fishing", I will let him go, or the labourer himself can
send a substitute. But if it is the day for threshing with the mill (I have a
steam mill), one day in the week, I generally want them to come that day.

'The oncas pay their rent to me and furnish the labour for me. I can
raise their rents. There is no exact number of days of labour stated: there
is nothing in my lease from the proprietor to stop me requiring it for

every lawful day of the year, if I wished, but I don't require it. I also have the power to dispossess any of them whenever I please; not in the middle of a year, however, because they hold from year to year. I have no intention at present to remove any, but if any of the crofts were clear, I could get half a dozen tenants who would gladly give the rent I ask, and endure all the bondage I put them under'.

'The Lairds of Harray'

As a county, Orkney has an exceptionally large number of landowners. Members of the Royal Commission were well aware of this before arriving in Orkney, thanks to the List of Proprietors of Lands and Heritages in Scotland, published in 1874. The number of people in Orkney who owned one acre or more was 762. This was two and a half times as many as in Shetland, which had 302 and is about one-third larger in area; and nine times as many as in Sutherland where there were 85 in a county six times bigger in area. Many small farmers in Orkney were 'peerie lairds' who owned their own farms and the Commission learned how important ownership was to a farmer when they met Peter Smith of Garth on the Mainland. He was one of 'the lairds of Harray'.

'My family have always lived in this place. I cannot tell you how long ago exactly the farm was purchased, but my predecessors have had it for upwards of 100 years. I have thirty-six acres arable, four or five acres of infield pasture, exclusive of commonty outside about twenty-six acres. The commonty was divided twenty years ago, but it isn't used as much as it used to be by cattle pasturing it.

'There has been a great improvement in the appearance of the properties and the methods of cultivation. The breed of cattle we keep is Shorthorn, as pure as we can. The land is all ploughed, not worked with

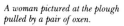
A woman pictured at the plough pulled by a pair of oxen.

the spade. We don't use oxen in ploughing, but they are used occasionally in small places. We raise some oats and barley, but no wheat. We use as much as we can of the grain for the family, and what we don't require we dispose of. We generally buy wheaten flour and use it along with the grain we raise ourselves.

'It is an advantage to be the proprietor of our own land but I have heard that sometimes the tenants of the Earl of Zetland are as well off as our Harray lairds. I don't suppose the Harray lairds would like to change with them, however; they would not want to leave certainty for hope. One would imagine the wish to become a proprietor is very general from the keen competition that takes place when a farm is for sale. I am not a married man but in general it is the eldest son who gets (succeeds to) the farm.

Burning kelp near the Earl of Orkney's palace, Birsay.

'In my little property, we always require hired servants. We hire them from year to year, and some of them have been with us a good many years. They are working people from the parish generally; their daughters more frequently hire out as servants than the daughters of the lairds'.

The minister of the parish, David Johnston, thought that possessing their own land and having no rent to pay stimulated them to greater industry. They were strongly attached to the soil and to their properties and he had seen a great improvement in their houses in the last fifteen years. They tended to intermarry very much and not seek wives outside their own district or class.

As an owner who had enough land, Peter Smith was not, strictly speaking, the kind of farmer Lord Napier's Commission was required to investigate but his example could influence them to recommend proprietorship of larger holdings as a desirable objective. But were they never, on their travels, to meet a tenant paying rent under £30 who had enough land to live off?

Crofter or small farmer?

When David Wallace of Bratsfold, Burness on Sanday gave evidence, he began unpromisingly by saying people in the parish had the usual grievances — 'high rent, no security of tenure, and no compensation for anything we do'. His own rent for 18¾ acres had risen at one swoop from £11 to £15 four years ago. He had improved the old croft all he could, taking in land from the waste, he said, and all the thanks he got was putting £4 on his rent, and he didn't like that. He thought £10 or £11 a fair rent, although he had to agree that having all his land together in one piece made it more convenient and therefore more valuable. Formerly, they had all held in *runrig*, which he described:

'In the old way the property was not squared, one had an acre and another had an acre. Then the property was squared and the rent was raised.

'I keep two horses, two cows, two two-year olds, two calves and four sheep. I am able to sell two two-year olds yearly and get perhaps £29 on an average for the two of them, and I sell two sheep for perhaps £4. The corn and other produce is all consumed on the farm. I don't buy any grain for living on; I can raise as much as does for the family. Yes, I really do pay my rent out of the animals I sell, the two two-year olds and the two sheep, but that does not mean I can always make ends meet: there are many other things besides rent.

'I don't do anything besides farming. I have no connection with fishing. I have a family but they go out to service and don't send any money to us. If I had more property I could support my parents or whatever it is, and lay by something for my old age, and not become a pauper myself. I would like a little more land but not a very large place'.

The Commissioners had found their man in David Wallace. When they asked him if he was a crofter, he replied, 'A small farmer'. When Charles Fraser MacKintosh enquired if he had been reading the newspaper reports of the Commission's meetings in other parts of the country and discovered that he had, he asked him, 'Do you think we often come upon people who get £29 for two beasts and £4 for two sheep, and have crops sufficient for themselves and their families without doing any other work? Have you seen any instance of that in the evidence you have read about the crofters?' David Wallace could only mumble, 'I could not say that; I could not say that I remember that', but the land he had in area and fertility, was what the bulk of the crofters in the west would have been happy to settle for as well.

Crofters in the West
Sutherland and Wester Ross

Having visited so many islands, the Royal Commissioners did not meet a single mainland crofter until the last week of July. Their first meeting on the west coast took place in the Free Church at Kinlochbervie and from here they worked their way south, calling in on communities on the shores of Sutherland, Wester Ross and Inverness-shire until they reached Lochaline in Morvern and visited the islands of Mull and Tiree. Travelling presented no difficulty. The *North Star* being entirely at their disposal, she was always ready to carry them on to their next meeting, which was usually on the next day in the next suitable church.

The great new problem they expected to encounter on the mainland was the large-scale expansion of deer forests. Fraser MacKintosh knew that in the north-west Highlands deer forests extended practically from sea to sea:

'From within a mile of Beauly railway station you can walk without putting a foot on anything but deer forest until you reach the Cro of Kintail. There are fourteen miles of deer forest in Glen Cannich, all the north side of Glen Affric, Balmacaan forest from Glen Urquhart and almost the whole of Guisachan, through to Glenshiel and from Invergarry House all the way down to the sea at Knoydart.'

Roderick Morrison, the minister of Kintail, wrote a paper on deer forests for the Royal Commission. His family had been the ministers in the parish for three generations, his grandfather having written the description of Kintail in the Old Statistical Account in 1792 and his father the one in the New Statistical Account in 1836. Looking at the area given over to deer in the Highlands in another way, Roderick Morrison reckoned that it was possible to walk from Loch Broom south to Fort William entirely over deer forest and from Loch Broom south-eastwards almost as far as Forfar.

Deer forest a greater evil than sheep?

He maintained that deer forest was the most unproductive use of land:

'The venison is not worth speaking of and is often left to rot on the ground, or thrown to dogs. Myriads of sheep and thousands of cattle were sent to market in former years from lands which now produce nothing whatever.

'Glen after glen is being cleared of its shepherd families who are replaced by one or two solitary game-watchers of "stoppers". These are usually the idlest of people pretending to earn a living, and the best customers of public houses and smugglers.

'We hear about the immense amount of money brought into the country by sportsmen — the "shower of gold" that annually falls on the Highlands. The large sums paid as rent are chiefly expended in London and elsewhere and the sporting tenants are only in the country for a few weeks in each year and as a rule take no interest in the state of the people'.

A stalking party setting out for the hill 1878.

The Camerons, a stalker's family at Kinlochmore dressed in their best for the photograph in the 1890s.

'Was it worse for crofters to live next to a deer forest'? the Commissioners asked Donald Munro of Strathan near Lochinver:

'It was a sheep farm', he told them, 'but it's only deer forest now, Glencanisp forest. It was made a forest two or three years ago, but it is not sufficiently fenced to keep the deer from getting into the crofts. They can go over it: it is only 3½ feet high. But it keeps our cattle from going over it — it is a barbed fence, to pierce any beast that tries, that is our belief.

Murdoch Kerr of Achmelvich, a crofter's son and road repairer, had no doubt that a sheep farm was a better neighbour to have than a deer forest:

'What good can we get out of deer?' he asked. 'The sheep are bad enough. They were the cause of the people being expelled from their places, but still they are better than deer. We can get no use of the deer, whereas if we can afford to buy a sheep, it will at all events provide us with clothes. As for the deer, we are not allowed to kill or eat them. The sheep need shepherds and there is some work connected with sheep for us in the way of smearing and shearing. But deer require no herd, and they can leap the fences and eat our crops. I don't know any work in connection with the deer except some gillies, perhaps.'

Challenged about having such a low fence between the deer forest and the crofts, the old Sutherland estate factor, Evander MacIver maintained that it was the kind of fence that was being erected now. It was not intended to be a deer fence, he said. He really didn't know if it would keep the deer out of the crofters' ground or not. Then he added, as if this new piece of information in some way answered the question, 'The Duke has put up the fence at his own expense'.

A crofting family near Poolewe about 1890.

Crofters at Deruner on Charles J. Murray's Lochcarron estate suffered even more from having deer as their neighbours. Their spokesman, Finlay MacBeath who had a family of six and only an acre and a quarter of arable to feed them on, claimed that their hill pasture which used to be big enough to feed a hundred and twenty sheep, had been swallowed up in the deer forest and now they were not allowed to keep a single sheep. Their township had no fence at all between their land and the deer. Donald MacLennan, the ground officer readily agreed that the deer destroyed their crops but, he said,

'The houses are dotted throughout the arable land here and there, and the people could watch the deer out of their beds. They have all families and one could be out and another in'.

Eventually he admitted that it was not a reasonable thing for crofters to have to sit up and keep awake all night to keep an eye on the deer. He thought the crops ought to be protected and undertook to speak to the new owner about a fence.

More hope in fishing?

Duncan MacKenzie came by boat from Reiff north of the Summer Isles to represent his township at Ullapool. He was 76 and he'd been a crofter for fifty years, but his family had left, 'taken wings and flown away', he said. Unusually, he brought no written statement of complaints with him. Instead he made a plea on behalf of forty young men in the place who had experience of fishing, because they needed help to buy bigger boats and gear, and a harbour where they could land their fish safely. The harbour they had was poor because it was open to the south-west wind and they had to haul their boats up on the shore for safety. He could not guarantee that with good boats and gear the young men could live by fishing alone but, he maintained, 'They could try whatever'. It was his belief that the land was for the old people and the sea for the young men but he agreed that they would be better to have a cow to give milk for their children and ground to grow their own potatoes rather than be buying them.

When he was asked about the state of their houses, Duncan replied, 'They would be none the worse of being better!' He had worked hard on the land he had, 2¼ acres of rocky and stony ground, even blasting the rocks but he couldn't even get an ounce of powder out of the proprietor. Improving the land did not pay the crofter in his experience — 'the man who improves best will have his rent increased most.'

Duncan MacKenzie had been a good witness, who had commonsense and a way with words but there were some things he would not tell, even when Sheriff Nicolson pressed him:

Sheriff: Have you any sheep?
Duncan: Yes.
Sheriff: How many?
Duncan: Indeed I have not many.
Sheriff: Perhaps you don't know how many?
Duncan: I know fine!
Sheriff: How many?
Duncan: Between five and ten.

Not what the factor put down in his Return!

Better a paid labourer than a crofter?

Alexander Grant, formerly a crofter, said he was now a labourer working for John Fowler at Braemore. John Fowler, a civil engineer, was well known for his work on the London Underground and had just begun what was to become the most famous engineering landmark in Scotland, the Forth Bridge (the railway bridge). He had had this estate for the last eighteen years. Alexander Grant had left his croft reluctantly: it was, he said, the dearest spot on earth to him but he had to go where he could get food and clothes. Now he had a house and potato ground for 1s.6d. a week (about £4 a year, as much as the rent of a croft) but he had regular work and was satisfied with his wages.

When asked if he preferred to be a labourer or a crofter, he quoted a Gaelic proverb in reply, 'The flagstone at the doorstep of the great house is slippery'. He meant that as a crofter he had had no security but this was followed up by a question on status, a leading question if ever there was one: 'Do you consider that as a crofter you had a higher social position than as a mere labourer?'

Alexander Grant replied, 'There was such a time but it is gone; now respect is given to the man that has means. When I had a croft I was a greater slave than I am now.'

Being an engineer, John Fowler appreciated the value of other men's skills. He did not think giving a man more land was necessarily a good thing if working it took him away from earning money at some trade, as a smith or a carpenter or a fisherman, or even as an unskilled labourer. He thought the construction of the railway up to Inverness had provided work for far more men and raised the level of wages, while the railway also allowed people to come into the Highlands and take country houses and shooting lodges, which they might wish to improve.

Labourers on A. G. Pirie's estate of Leckmelm in 1883.

ROYAL COMMISSION (HIGHLANDS AND ISLANDS.)
RETURN RESPECTING COTTARS
on the Estate of *Leckmelm - Co. Ross* the Property of *A. G. Pirie Esq* as at the 1st day of January 1883.
1.   2.   3.   4.   5.

No.	NAME.	Residence, whether on a Croft, or not on a Croft.		Rent, if any.			Occupation or Means of Subsistence.
		On a Croft.	Not on a Croft.	Amount. £ s. d.		To whom paid, Proprietor or Tenant.	
1	Colin Mackenzie		not	2 12 0		Proprietor	Yachtsman
2	Alex. Campbell		Do.	1 10 0		Do.	Merchant
3	John Maclean		Do.	0 12 0		Do.	Dyker & labourer on the Estate
4	Theos. Macleod		Do.	0 12 0		Do.	Labourer on Estate
5	Simon Mackenzie		Do.	0 12 0		Do.	Do.
6	John Mackenzie		Do.	0 12 0		Do.	Do.
7	John Cameron		Do.	0 12 0		Do.	Do.
8	Roderick Mackenzie		Do.	0 12 0		Do.	Do.
9	Donald Campbell		Do.	0 12 0		Do.	Dyker & labourer on the Estate
10	Alex. Maclean		Do.	0 12 0		Do.	Labourer on Estate

Signed *C. R. Manners*
Address *12 Southend St. Inverness*
Date *May 21st 1883*

He needed workers on his estate because he was making roads and bridges and improving the land by trenching. The rate of wages he was paying that summer was 3s. a day for efficient labour, and sometimes 2s.6d. a day. Being asked how crofters compared as labourers with workmen in other parts of the country — an awkward question to answer in a meeting full of crofters — he replied:

'Men of the crofting class have not the same continuous training for any work, or the strong food of what may be called the navvy class who do the work on the railways, and whose sole business it is. I don't say that in the way of finding fault with the crofter class, because their occupation is a different one; but a crofter at 3s. a day would be at least as expensive as an English navvy at 4s.6d.'

He had spent about £105,000 on the estate since he came and he had always employed workers living in the district if he possibly could. He had no intention of preventing crofters on the estate from continuing to be crofters. In this he was unlike A. G. Pirie, the new owner of Leckmelm nearer to Ullapool, who took the land of his crofters in with his own farm and gave them paid work instead. Some of them became farmworkers, some gardeners, some tree-planters, and other gillies or yachtsmen. Of course, Pirie admitted, the men would rather have been able to keep their land and have work and wages as well.

The MacKenzies have their say

Sir Kenneth MacKenzie of Gairloch did not sit as one of the Commissioners at the meeting in Poolewe to allow the delegates who were his tenants, to feel free to speak their minds.

Alexander MacKenzie, a carpenter-crofter in Strath, Gairloch explained about compulsory labour, his chief complaint:

'We do sixty hours in the year, and receive no wages and no food. If it is inconvenient for anyone to give the labour himself, he can find a substitute, of course at his own expense, perhaps 2s.6d. or 3s. a day. The work is chiefly upon the roads, the branch roads which lead to our crofts, and some of it repairing the march fences between ourselves and the big farmers. (One man had to keep the mill dam in repair.) If a crofter brings his horse, he gets off with three days instead of six'.

Sir Kenneth MacKenzie's manager, Donald MacKenzie, found the people not very willing to do this work. They didn't come out early in the morning; in practice they didn't work thirty hours, and a great many didn't work at all. Sir Kenneth provided the supervision and the tools and was responsible for the bridges, he said, and what was done benefited the crofters themselves.

Another Alexander MacKenzie, one of three with that name in Midtown of Inverasdale, told tales of factors in the past seizing cattle for £1 of arrears of rent, but he praised the present proprietor, Sir Kenneth MacKenzie, for his great kindness to the people, especially widows and orphans, many of whom held land rent free. He wished Sir Kenneth would reside more frequently in Gairloch so that he would know about everything better. 'We know him very well and we see him once a year', he said, 'and we'd like it better if we were seeing him always. He speaks the language of the people (Gaelic) but perhaps not so well as he would wish!'

South Erradale was full of MacKenzies: out of sixteen families there twelve were MacKenzies, including three Johns as heads of the household and two Kenneths. One of the Kenneths, then aged 44 complained particularly about the hill pasture:

'It would have been better if one half of it had been a sheet of water. It is a very unhealthy place for stock, full of peat haggs, where they are

Cattle and people by some abandoned houses at Poolewe.

drowned. Everybody that has a croft has the right to put a beast on this pasture. The rate we pay is 6s. for every cow, 3s. for a stirk and 1s.3d. for a sheep, but a calf or a lamb goes free.

'There is a place near us that we would like in the deer forest which marches with our own hill pasture. It is very good sheep ground: there is no comparison between the two'.

Osgood Hanbury MacKenzie of Inverewe was later to gain fame for the garden he created at Inverewe and the book he wrote, *A Hundred Years of the Highlands.* Already he was busy planting trees. 'If I had more money, I should like to plant thousands of acres,' he said, 'but it is rather expensive work. Timber has also given a good deal of employment in Gairloch for many years, for roofing and fence posts. Everybody wants fences now, even the crofters.

'But there is little other employment for the people, except for a short time when the shooting tenants are here. Some of them have gardeners, and some men are boatmen for the fishermen. The tourists also give them a fair market for eggs and poultry, and help to raise the prices.

An old man on then and now

Duncan MacRae was 87. He was one of seventeen crofters at Sallachy on Loch Long north of Dornie and he'd been there nearly sixty years. He came from Kyle Rhea in Kintail but there were no people left in Kintail now, he said, only deer.

'We have a school and I believe the children all go to school. They are coming on very well at reading and writing. He is an honest fellow, the schoolmaster. They are better scholars: there were no scholars at all sixty years ago.

'People are finer clothed but not so well fed. I was fed on milk and the produce of sheep, goats, cows, cattle and fish. Now they are fed on potatoes and herring, bread and tea, but they have no butter and no cheese. They also eat more meal now, six times more.

'Many of them are becoming rascals today. I believe they were formerly more friendly than they are today and more cheery. They were spending a good deal of their time in each other's houses and telling stories. It was a nice way of spending time in the winter nights. They would be twisting ropes and the women would be spinning in the evenings. There is no word of that today.

'They made their own blankets and every stitch that they put on, but they make very little now, because wool has been so dear. Everybody made his own shoes: there was no shoemaker at all when I first mind.

'There was plenty playing on the pipes, but there's very little now. Sometimes they took too much whisky. There was a parish church and there was a Roman Catholic church always too in Kintail. People did not go so regularly as they do now. They didn't play games on a Sunday but they went among their cattle and wandered on the hills. Now on the whole they behave themselves better, and pay more regard to the Sabbath especially.

'Yes, I've heard my people talking about the battle of Sheriffmuir (which was in 1715). My father's brother went to Sheriffmuir and never came home. It was in Prince Charlie's time. I'm quite sure it was my father's brother who was at Sheriffmuir, not my grandfather's brother. My father was about eighty when he died: that was about fifteen years ago. I knew several old soldiers who had been at Waterloo. One especially used always to be in our house, being a relative, and he was quite contented. For myself, I've always been as happy as I am now; yes, and more so.'

Curiosity

Two old crofters had travelled fifteen miles from Cuaig in the north-west of the Applecross peninsula to be in the big audience in the parish church at Shieldaig. They were Donald MacRae, who was also a tailor, and his friend John MacLennan. They knew Alexander Livingstone of Fearnbeg well, the man who was telling the Commissioners about the difficulties of the four hundred people in north Applecross, the children not able to get to school, the postman having to scramble over streams and he as a seller of goods going from township to township by boat, all for want of a road. (Only in 1976 did north Applecross get a road but by then nearly all of the people had gone.) When Lord Napier asked Donald MacRae why he was at Shieldaig that day, he replied, 'To see what was going on'. Then hearing that John MacLennan also had nothing to say, Lord Napier asked him why he had come and John had told him, 'Just to see what you were all doing here.' 'Are you satisfied?' asked Lord Napier. 'Yes'. said John and then he went on, 'Well, the deer come and eat our crops . . .'.

Challenge and response

Questioning Sir Alexander Matheson's factor at Balmacara about how little of the money laid out on the Kintail estate was spent on improvements to benefit the crofters, Lord Napier was suddenly interrupted when from the body of the church, Sir Alexander Matheson burst out, 'I want to end this discussion by making a statement.' 'Excuse me', said the chairman, 'will you have the great kindness then to come and sit down here?'

'I only wish to say a few words,' Sir Alexander Matheson retorted.

'Then,' Lord Napier insisted, 'I would wish you would rather do it as any other witness,' and waited for him to be seated in the witness's chair before allowing a short statement on his estate policy on crofters. He wanted to have tenants of all descriptions. None of his farms was huge, the rents were all below £500 a year, as many as possible were between £50 and £100 a year and ranged down to people in club farms paying £20 a year each but he was not in favour of little crofts, if there was other employment for the people to make a living by:

'At this moment,' he declared, 'I consider we have rather too many of that class in Lochalsh, and I would be glad if some of them would leave and better themselves elsewhere. I would be glad if half of them would go to America or somewhere.'

Crofters in the West
Inverness-shire and Argyll

At Glenelg the Commissioners heard first how the land of the people who went to Canada about 1850 was all turned into sheep farms. Then the minister, James MacDonald, reinforced the descriptions the crofters who remained had been giving of their own condition.

'The people are poor. Generally they have need of increase of grazing and they would be the better of some additional land. I also know a little about Lewis (his wife was the daughter of the minister of Stornoway) and I believe the people of Lewis are better off than the crofters here. They have more outlet for hill grazing and more land, and have access to sea-manure, in the greater part of Lewis. They are also larger crofters in Lewis.

'Even the fishing in Loch Hourn is very uncertain. It is not good fishing ground for anything else but herring; and along the coast of Lewis they have very good general fishing for the rest of the year, and herring at the season'.

On the other hand when Lord Napier mentioned being struck by the want of any partition between a family and its cattle in houses in Lewis, and by people and cattle entering by the same door in Skye, the minister said he was not aware of any houses like these in Glenelg.

Little chance to work for wages

Glenelg being an area where not only the landlords were absentees but also the tenant-farmers, crofters who were tradesmen could find little employment locally. Donald MacPherson, a joiner of Kirkton, Glenelg had had to go across to the Isle of Skye to work for the last twenty-three years, and Donald Stewart of Little Galltair, a blacksmith found that sheep farms did not have much work for a blacksmith to do. And even to get pasture for the young beasts they wanted to keep, they had to send *them* to Skye!

Because there was no paid work in South Morar either, Colin MacDonald of Bunacaimb, a township where every one of the 42 inhabitants was a MacDonald, said the men went to the Loch Hourn fishing:

'It is the only thing we have had to depend on for the last eight years. We make very little in cod and ling fishing. We don't go very often, only if we think we can make any money by it. But we've been successful in the herring fishing, particularly the last two years. If the herring fishing proves a failure, we have to turn to gathering whelks to pay our rent. The women gather them, and the men if the herring fishing fails. We get 8s. or 10s. per bag for them and they go to London. A woman would gather about a bag in a week and could save say 8s. in the week. They can only gather them when the tide is out, about five days in a fortnight at spring tides'.

Another family, Donald MacVarish's at Ardnish, not far from where 'Bonnie Prince Charlie' had landed and departed, only started gathering them when every other occupation had failed. Donald, a 64-year-old crofter, said it had become 'our best source of income'. They were at it from after harvest in autumn until the spring, but the crop was diminishing and in five or six days of a spring tide a picker had to work well to earn about 5s. Men, women and children all gathered whelks but, said Donald, 'It is very hard work for the men'. When Sheriff Nicolson asked him if it wasn't harder for the women and children, he replied, 'They don't complain of it so much'!

The jobs they had lost in his area were droving and smearing sheep:

'*Smearing* sheep (with a salve of tar and butter) has gone out of fashion. There is only one man smearing now for every twelve that used to be.

We used to drive herds of cattle and sheep to Falkirk and other markets and we sometimes made £14 to £15 by that in the season. That source of income is lost to us now since the railways are opened. I know the nearest station is far from here and the sheep have still to be driven there. A shepherd with perhaps one or two attendants can drive the stock to Banavie, and then they ship them from there (along the Caledonian Canal), and sometimes they drive them to Tyndrum and put them on the Oban railway, or Kingussie on the Highland line.'

Another way of crofting — the club farm

Charles Cameron, who was 65 and one of the five crofters of Acharacle in Ardnamurchan explained that each of them could keep four cows and a horse on his own lot and they had 100 sheep which they held in common on the hill. It had been a club farm ever since he could remember:

'There is one mark for all the sheep which belong to all the tenants in common. One of us is chosen to go and sell the stock, and whatever he gets we are all agreeable to it. We get as much for the wool as pays for the smearing of the sheep, and sometimes a little over, and we sell perhaps thirty or forty lambs and a few aged sheep at the end of the season'.

The Acharacle crofters found the club system worked well for them but it did not make them rich. Because their rents were high, £18 a year, they had to take any work they could, such as ploughing for smaller crofters. Charles Cameron also relied on his grown-up daughter's earnings in England — 'What she is able to give me helps to pay my rent and,' he added, 'to support me.'

Very poor people

The Commission encountered many people who were frightened of poverty in their old age. One of them, Donald MacDonald was nearly 80, the oldest of the three crofters at Polnish on the Arisaig estate.

'Two of us pay 30s. a year and one pays £2 for mere shells of black houses which we thatch ourselves; the rent was only 6d. till the last repair was made four years ago, and for a cow's grass apiece we pay £3 to the tacksman. From being poor we have become poorer and our case is really pitiable. Our demands are not great — as much land as would afford us summering and wintering for a cow, and land in which to plant a few potatoes, and to be protected from the deer above all things.'

People on the Arisaig and South Morar estate were worried by new estate regulations, which they called 'The Seventeen Commandments' affecting not only the crofter's relations with the landlord but also with his own children. John MacEachran who was 70 and lived in Back of Keppoch found one of the rules particularly hard: sons and daughters on reaching 21, whether married or not, were bound to go and live elsewhere. That rule would deprive people like him of help in their old age:

'It is the young who support the old. This almost compels the father to curse his son, and send him out of his house, saying, "Walk out with you and let me see your face no more", when the son arrives at the age of twenty-one. Indeed yes, I believe all the married sons should be allowed to remain with their wives in their father's house.'

Others cleared from places like Knock on the Morvern estate in 1866 into the village of Lochaline, could look ahead with little hope. Able-bodied men like Alexander Cameron who spoke for them survived by finding work elsewhere, in his case as a mason's labourer at Ardtornish, but the older people, without relatives or land for a cow, 'just had to go on the parish, and shortly after that', he said, 'they died'.

Thatched house and outhouse at Caoles on Tiree in 1973.

Crofters and Cottars in Tiree

Landing in Tiree in bright sunshine, the Commissioners found a large crowd waiting to cheer them and accompany them to the church of John Gregorson Campbell the authority on Celtic folk-lore. The size of their audience was exceptional: out of an island population of about 2700, between 700 and 800 people crowded in. Small wonder on such a warm day that workmen had to come and take out one window of the church completely and force another one open!

The people were tenants of the Duke of Argyll. The landscape of their low fertile island reminded the *Scotsman* reporter of the small farms he'd seen on Sanday in Orkney. John MacFadyen of Caoles at the east end was typical of the crofters in the bigger crofts. There were twenty in his township, each with about twelve acres of arable, too little, he said, to allow a rotation of crops, and they had to buy in a lot of meal.

'We grind some barley some years', he said, 'but we have more than enough to do after feeding the stock to sow down crop again. Most of us give to the cattle the whole of the barley and oats but there are others who send something to the mill. Of course the potatoes always go to the family. We raise fifty to sixty barrels of potatoes in an average year off an average croft. For ourselves we use probably between thirty and forty barrels and we sell the rest out of the island.'

Hearing that he kept two horses on only twelve acres of arable, Sir Kenneth MacKenzie expressed astonishment, thinking they would eat too much of the produce of the croft, but John MacFadyen insisted that one horse wouldn't do and sharing with a neighbour didn't work:

'We cannot do with one horse. The ground is light and sandy and some of it is mossy. It must be ploughed quick and sown when it is ploughed. I've tried keeping two horses between us and we could not get on with it. My neighbour might have other work to do with the horse, like carrying sea-ware when I would like to be at the plough'.

The lives of the cottars were very different, as Hector MacDonald, a 38-year-old cottar at Balemartine at the other end of the island explained:

'There are thirty-two cottar families at Balemartine, some who were put out of Hillipool (the factor's sheep farm) before I was born. They built houses on the seashore on the common belonging to Balemartine. Our ordinary employment is fishing but for want of a safe harbour, we have to use very small boats.

No, we have no land whatever, not even a bit for potatoes — not the breadth of the soles of our feet!

We live by fishing, for cod, ling, lobsters. Some send it to Glasgow and some sell it at the shops. We get £26,10s. to £28,10s. per ton for ling, £23 per ton for cod, that is for dried salt fish, but we don't fish for herrings; we have no herring boats. Yes, there are here present a great number of young strong men but many others are away. Some are at the east coast fishing, some on board steamers, some in all quarters of the earth, but I believe the greater portion of our livelihood is taken out of the sea round this coast here.'

By asking John MacFadyen the Commission established that roughly half the land in Tiree was given over to six large sheep farms and that practically all the people were living on the other half. The only new provider of work for them was the North British Chemical Company, which made iodine out of seaweed at their main factory in Clydebank.

The manager explained that they employed only a few men directly in Tiree, carters and three or four others when the factory was working, but they paid other people for the heaps of sea tangle they gathered. This was mainly winter work when spring tides drove it up on the shore and men, women and children gathered it and carried it on their backs to make heaps out of reach of the sea. Donald Sinclair of Balphail reckoned his sister, a widow, and her three children went out gathering with him even at night and even in winter. That was customary all over the place, he said, then they might get no more for a month. He complained about the way they were paid, in goods in the Company's store instead of in money but the manager defended the system because it was difficult for him to get money on an island which had no bank.

Cottars on Lochshiel estate, signs of a kindlier landlord.

ROYAL COMMISSION (HIGHLANDS AND ISLANDS.)

RETURN respecting CROFTERS and COTTARS on the Estate of *Lochshiel* in the Property of *Lord Howard of Glossop* as at the 1st day of Januar

No.	Name of Tenant Cottars	Number of Families residing on Croft.	Number of Persons habitually residing	Number of separate Dwelling Houses on Croft.	Rent of Croft including Grazing Rights, in Money.	Obligations &c.	Extent of Arable Land in Imperial Acres and fractions of an Acre.	Extent of Pasture Land individually held in Acres, if any.	Number estimated to be kept.			Number actually kept.		
					£ s. d.				Horses of all ages.	Cattle. Above / Under	Sheep of all ages.	Horses of all ages.	Cattle. Above / Under	Sheep of all ages.
1	Ann McDonald	—	2	—	No rent	Has Cottage, Cowhouse, some potato ground, and grazing for her Cattle	—		1 / 1	—	—	1 / 1	—
2	Roderick McDonald	—	6	—		Cottage & land for Potatoes Oats & grazing for her Cattle			1 / 1	—	—	1 / 1	—
3	Allan McDonald	—	6	—		Cottage some potato ground & grazing for one Cow	—		1	—	—	1	—
4	Peggy Mackenzie	—	1			" Cottage & piece of land	—						
5	Duncan McMillan on John McGrigors Croft No 4 Sheet 1 & pays him £1·1·8 for grazing one of the Cows entered as McGregor's												
6	Peggy McVarich	—	1			Cottage Pauper	—						
7	Ann McDonald }					Do	Do						
8	Mary McDonald }	— 2	—	—									
9	James McGillivray	—		—	5·	Blacksmith House & Smithy	—						
10													

'Improvement' and the people in Mull

Lachlan Kennedy, the carrier in Dervaig in the north of Mull, explained that the people had built their own houses with stone and lime in the village and roofed them with thatch, but by 1883 most of the houses were slated. Each householder had a garden of a quarter of an acre, a croft and the hills of Monabeg and Torr as pasture, and between them they were able to keep fifty-six cows, a bull and twenty-eight horses. Intent on 'improvement' the new owner took Monabeg in order to plough it up, promising to give it back in three years, but the rent he wanted was far too high for them. Then he took away the hill of Torr and they, without grazing, had to sell their animals to his manager at nominal prices. Without stock their standard of living and way of life changed:

'We could no longer manure in a proper manner and our produce decreased. At present a crofter can have little meal off his own croft. The expense of working our crofts, engaging horses for ploughing, harrowing and carting manure is considerable. One of our small crofts will take between 30s. and 40s. for the said work. Peats we have to carry 1¼ mile on our back, or pay 1s.3d. for each cart which most of us cannot afford.'

The other delegate for Dervaig, John Campbell was an ex-soldier who had been through the Crimean War and the Indian Mutiny. When he was asked if many young men from Mull joined the army today, he replied, 'Bless you, no. There are no men in our parish — nothing but sheep and game.'

Meeting in their Temperance Hall in Salen to prepare the case they would put to the Royal Commission, the crofters and cottars on the Glenforsa estate were asked a series of questions:

'How many of you present have enough of land?'
Not a hand was raised.
'How many are there who have not enough of land?'
All hands went up.
'How many on the estate of Glenforsa have enough land to live on?'
'Two'.
'How has it come about that there are so few holding land enough, and so many having so little?'
'The people have been cleared off excellent and extensive lands and sent hither and thither, some settling in Salen, some in Tobermory, some in Glasgow and some in foreign lands'.

As an example, they said the island of Ulva had had a population of 859 in 1841. (That was the population of the parish, whereas the island contained 604 people in 1837.) Lachlan MacQuarrie, now 64 and living in Salen said there were now on the island only the proprietor, and his three shepherds, besides two or three cottars. At first he himself had a large croft on Ulva at Ormaig but someone offered more rent and he had to move to a smaller croft at Cragaig. Evicted from there with his wife and three young children he had taken the couples of his house and built a hut with them on the shore. It was so close to highwater mark that the proprietor on seeing it gave him a house at £3 a year at Caolos and he had lived by catching lobsters. When he left there it was of his own accord.

'Yes, I remember when Ulva belonged to the MacQuarries (until 1835). People were comfortable then, and they were comfortable in my time. It is a pretty fertile island for raising oats and potatoes but there is no crop at all now, except what the laird grows himself'.

Farewell to the west

Fortunately, the Royal Commission's journey along the west coast was blessed with fine weather day after day until they reached Mull. Then a great storm blew up with winds of hurricane force, driving rain and even sleet — all this in early August! The meeting they had arranged in Iona had to be cancelled because there was no chance of landing but this was almost the only disappointment on their cruise. They had sailed 1100 miles on board the *North Star* with Captain Ritchie, whom they had learned to regard as a very fine seaman. Strangely, one of the witnesses who appeared before them at Tobermory was John MacDonald, master

For years the Temperance Hall in Tobermory, where the Royal Commission met, set its face against strong drink but as the notice shows it is losing the battle.

mariner, who had been their pilot on the *Lively*. No mention was made of that unfortunate ship. Instead the Commissioners took the opportunity to enlist the exceptional knowledge he had of western harbours and record in detail what he advised on the best places to build piers and the size of boats that would be needed to allow west coast fishermen to compete on equal terms with the east coast men.

And return

No greater proof of the dedication of this Royal Commission can be cited than the extra meeting it held in Tarbert, Loch Fyne. The time was the day after Christmas 1883 and the purpose was to see if there were lessons to be learned from these herring fishermen which would help others on the west coast. Hugh Carmichael who was 40, told them about his kind of fishing:

Loch Fyne fishermen at their stance with a skiff.

'I am a fisherman with no croft or field, just a small cottage and garden. Very few fishermen here have crofts, perhaps half a dozen. They work them partly themselves, and their families, but they do not remain home from the fishing to work their crofts. With the Loch Fyne fishing as it is at present they would do as well without crofts.

'The fishing has improved very much. The first reason is that there are screw steamers plying between here and Glasgow, and we get a better price now, double what it used to be. There is also more fish landed now in the village, owing to the trawling system. We begin to fish in May and go on till December. Then a good number of fishermen go over to the Ayrshire shore about the beginning of January for a couple of months.

Then they are at home and prepare their nets and boats for the beginning of May.

'It is *skiffs* we use here. We have got them larger now; this year or two back some have been getting what they call decks and they can live on them now. We consider them quite large enough at twenty-four to twenty-six feet keel to be handled with oars to pull the *trawl* instead of sail. Yes, the trawl may through time come to be worked by steamers. I used to fish in the days of drift nets but they are nearly given up, especially at Tarbert. The trawl is a great advantage to the fishermen and for the market too. They get the fish earlier because we pull the trawl in earlier and we fish in daylight too. There are screws at hand ready to take them to Glasgow and the fish can be got there for the Glasgow folk to eat that day. They reach Glasgow in five hours and discharge at the Broomielaw.

'Each boat has one trawl net, 90 fathoms long and 18 fathoms deep and two boats always work together. When they come across a shoal of herrings, the one boat shoots round the shoal and each boat pulls in its own net. Then, when the net is at the stern, they lift it out of the water and take the fish into the boat. There is a sole rope to the bottom of the net so that we can make a complete circle. Usually we draw to the shore: it's the surer way to catch the fish.

'We should have a close time with no fishing between sunset on Saturday and sunrise on Monday. Fishermen from Campbeltown fish on the Sabbath and we in Tarbert are at a great disadvantage in this. I don't think this is a religious question: I think those who do it have no religion at all. We would like to get the rest; and the herrings would come in to the shore better if they got quiet from Saturday till Monday morning.

'Loch Fyne has always been a good place for herring, very sheltered. The herring have never left it, and there's no fear that they will, so far as we can judge.

'There is double the population in the town now than there was twenty years ago, people growing up in the place mainly, very few strangers. Fishermen live to a good age in Tarbert. In former years people had not boats and material in as good order as at present. Seeing they are improving in the matter of oilskins and keeping themselves drier, that might be a reason why the fishing might have affected their health in former times. So, they will get older in the future.

'The inhabitants are well-to-do, because the fishing has been good these five years back. There are sixty-seven trawling skiffs in the village. They are always between four men. Each boat has four men and each man has a share of both boat and nets. They all belong to themselves. The boats are built here, each is worth between £60 and £70 and a complete set of nets or trawls, which we get from Kilbirnie or Paisley, costs about £35 or £40, say £35'.

Another fisherman, Archibald Paterson, supported him explaining that having a share in the boat made Tarbert men work harder:

'Anybody that works here can only work in a company of four, so that the boats and nets are among the four, and Jack is as good as his master. When we are working it is for ourselves, and we do our best to make a living. We are much better off than a man sailing from Glasgow or Greenock.'

Thanks to two advantages, the more predictable behaviour of the herrings in Loch Fyne and the proximity of the vast Glasgow market, fishing out of Tarbert, the Commissioners learned, was a profitable alternative to crofting, which pointed the way to a different, more equal social structure.

Crofters in the North and East

Bettyhill at the mouth of the Naver was the place chosen for the meetings on the north coast. When the Commissioners were unable to land any closer than Scrabster on the first morning, the necessity of driving thirty miles along to Bettyhill gave them the opportunity to identify between the road and the shore the little communities which had become so crowded —Melvich, Port Skerra, Strathy, Strathy Point, Armadale, Kirtomy and Farr — names which rang in the story of the Sutherland clearances. The audience awaiting them at the Free Church of Farr was largely made up of descendants of the people cleared out of Strathnaver and contained one or two veterans as well.

Young men and old on the clearances

The first young man to address them, Adam Gunn, who was described as a crofter's son, referred to some of these places directly. Before the clearances, he said, there had been only four crofters in Strathy and now there were forty-two, over twenty of them from Strathnaver alone; and at Armadale where formerly there were seven, there were now over thirty. Small wonder that their crofts were far too small and had not nearly enough hill pasture. If they had a proper harbour at Port Skerra, where besides thirteen cottar families there were 273 people living on very small crofts, they could be more successful as fishermen. Then clutching at another remedy Fraser MacKintosh floated before him, he thought it would be a good thing for the Strathnaver people if the Duke were to send them all back to Strathnaver!

Ruins at Grummore on Loch Naver, Sutherland, emptied in the clearance in 1819.

When Lord Napier asked him if he had any other occupation besides agricultural labourer, Adam Gunn replied, 'Yes, I'm a student at St Andrews'. (He was a Free Church minister at Durness five years later.)

The next time another very young witness appeared, Lord Napier established by his first question that he too was a student studying divinity, as well as a crofter's son. He was Angus MacKay of Cattlefield, Farr, later to become a Free Church minister in Caithness. He used much more colourful language to describe how his people came to be in such a poor place and condition:

'We and our fathers have been cruelly burnt like wasps out of Strathnaver, and forced down to the barren rocks of the seashore, where we had in many cases to carry earth on our backs to form a patch of land. Now, after we have improved the land, at our own expense, and built houses, our rents are raised at every opportunity — always when the head of a family dies and a new name is put on the rent roll.

'The land our forefathers lived on so happy and prosperous is now under deer and sheep and turning into moss and fog, while we are huddled together in small townships on the shore exposed to all the fury of the wild North Sea breezes, which generally carry away the little corn we have. I have heard from my forefathers about their prosperity in Strathnaver and it is the common talk of the people who have been in Strathnaver, who saw the doings and the burning of it. They had more land and more flesh and more fish and the like of that, but they were not given so much to work in the south then as now. I think they were pretty well off in Strathnaver; it was one of the best straths in Sutherland.'

Crofts at Farr.

Another Angus MacKay who was eighty lived at Strathy Point, where nineteen out of the twenty-seven families of crofters were MacKays. Angus came to tell how he remembered life in Strathnaver and how the people were cleared:

'If you were going up the strath now you would see on both sides of it the places where the townships were. There were four or five families in each township and bonnie haughs between them, and hill pasture for miles, as far as they could wish to go. The people had plenty of flocks of goats, sheep, horses, and cattle, and they were living happy. Remarkably comfortable — that's what they were — with flesh and fish and butter and cheese and fowl and potatoes and kail and milk too. There was no want of anything with them; and they had the Gospel preached to them at both ends of the strath'.

He did not say where his family were living at the time of the first removal when he was eleven, but they moved a mile and a half only down to the wood of Skail. Early that morning his father, mother and brother went away with their cattle and sheep, a horse, two mares and two foals and, he said, they left him and the younger children in bed. Later, carrying his brother across the river, he slipped in deep water and a woman had to jump in and save them from drowning. This had such an effect on him that when asked about houses being set on fire, he agreed that a number were 'from the river Owenmalloch and another river coming into Strathnaver on the east side, down to Dunviden Burn', but he did not remember seeing them burning — 'That is said but I cannot say; I saw nothing because my friends dried me and put me to bed.'

Thomas Purves of Rhifail who also farmed in Caithness was one of the sheep farmers who moved into Strathnaver. He travelled to Inverness to appear before the Commission to contradict old Angus' story. He insisted that Angus was living on the opposite side of the river from where the burning was, and that in trying to cross the river, he was heading for the burning party. Then, putting it another way he said, 'He was on the side where the burning was not going on'. Here was evidence surely that in Thomas Purves' mind there was no doubt that evictions by burning did take place, and when he was given the opportunity later to go the length of saying that there never was any burning, he replied that he would not.

Angus' other childhood memories were his father building a new house for them using feal (turf) and no stone at all, and that after five years they were removed a second time to Strathy Point. He had no wish now to return to Strathnaver:

'What would I do there? Nothing at all. I want nothing but raiment and daily bread, if the Lord provide that for me'.

The Commissioners, however, did want to drive through Strathnaver to see it for themselves and when they left, the people cheered them on their way.

Caithness crofters

No cheers greeted them in Caithness, however, when they arrived by train on 4th October because many people resented only one day being allocated to their large agricultural county. Some were uncertain about the place of meeting, thinking it was to be Bruan on the Clyth estate, not Lybster six miles farther south, and the cheering which did break out in Lybster that morning was for the crofters who had walked in a body from Bruan.

Speaking for the working farmers and crofters James Waters of Bower named several estates which had cleared out all the crofters and cottars. Up near Castletown on Mr Traill of Rattar's property, however, a good many people (53 families) were allowed to hold on to small crofts, just big enough to keep a cow — and with good reason, he said.

'They are employed as labourers in his pavement quarries. These poor workmen must have milk and must submit to be rack-rented. They are only paid once in three or four months, their wages only being 2s. to 2s.4d. per day of ten hours. They are, most of them, over head and ears in debt. The great bulk of them are compelled to take their meal out of the laird's store, and they must also take their coals from him at any price he likes to charge. They pay high rent for their crofts, £2 to £3 for their houses and also £2 for cow's grass. No wonder the poor workmen are so miserably poor and so deeply in debt.'

On the Clyth estate at Bruan the complaint was the exceptionally high rents, recently raised again by the absentee landlord. George Cormack had one of these crofts, eleven acres arable and about five more he had broken in, but his rent was £24 and they had had no common grazing for thirty years. He described the part the crofters had played in making their little farms under a plan by Sinclair of Ulbster in 1855 to make new lots and build new houses.

'The old zigzag (runrig) lots were cut up and on some of the new lots there were as many as five old houses and on others none. The tenant who would remove the old houses and dykes, build a new house and steading and fill up ditches would get a lease of fourteen years and £5 for building a dwellinghouse. The proprietor would give slate and flag at the Clyth quarry and lime for pointing. Believing it was for our good and comfort we worked hard until seventy slated houses and seventy-three thatched houses and steadings were built, and the remaining houses well repaired. These improvements greatly improved the appearance of the estate and he sold the estate to the present proprietor in 1862–63, who began by raising the rents.

Caithness flag used on the north coast for roofing and walling.

'I keep one horse, three cows, three calves and two sheep, and at Martinmas this season I will have to sell off some of the calves. I will thresh my grain in our own barn and grind it at the mill. We are bound to go to that mill with all the corn we convert into meal, and pay 1½d. per boll more than we can get it done for elsewhere. In a very good season the grain may do the family who are not very old. The oldest is only nine. Potatoes are not a very poor crop on our side of the coast. They don't agree well with the salt spray that is dashed up'.

'I also have a large share in a boat', he said, 'and if I can take the rent out of the sea, I can stay then in the winter comfortably'.

Obviously the other five men and the boy in his crew, being hired hands with little or no share in the boat, could expect less comfortable winters and the number of men with shares in a boat was diminishing. Rents on the estate were higher than the rest of the county anyway because it had so many creeks and harbours; and people cleared out of Sutherland who came to settle there as fishermen had to agree to high

A small-holding at Laidhay, Dunbeath, Caithness, the house in the middle, the byre at this end, the stable at the far end.

rents before building a house and breaking in a little bit of ground for themselves.

He had not heard of large farms in Caithness having cottar families on them, like the oncas in Orkney, who were compelled to do the work of the farm. Big farmers went to the hiring markets and hired workers usually for twelve months, from the men and women who came looking for work. A big farmer and writer of *The Agriculture of Caithness*, James Purves believed the great range in the size of farms in Caithness benefited the crofter, buying up his calves for fattening, for example, and providing jobs on the farm for his sons and daughters.

When Adam Sharp, the owner of Clyth, was given the chance to reply, his answers were booed or hissed or laughed at by the audience. Never on their travels so far had the Royal Commission encountered such a vocal and partisan assembly as this, determined to play an active part by expressing its disapproval of any statements in favour of landlords. Twice earlier when factors were speaking, the chairman had issued a warning that if necessary he would suspend the sitting and in the prolonged noise after Adam Sharp sat down, he brought proceedings to a close for the day.

Crofts for men who enlisted

The view was commonly held in Sutherland that if a crofter's son enlisted in the 93rd (Sutherland) Highlanders he was told his father's croft would be there for him on his return. If such a promise was made, it is a pity it was not put in writing, as John Sutherland of Muie in Rogart discovered:

'As an inducement to my father to enlist in the 93rd Highlanders, my grandfather got a promise of being left undisturbed in his lot during his lifetime, and if his son survived the term of his service, he would succeed him. My father joined that regiment and was wounded at New Orleans. On the expiry of his service in the army he returned home and expected to succeed his father as tenant of the whole lot but, to make room for another man who was evicted from a sheep farm, my father was summonsed and deprived of the best part of his father's lot. He was offered about two acres on the outskirts of his lot, on which we had to build new houses. I reclaimed, mostly by my own labour, nearly all the land I have'.

The factor, Joseph Peacock, insisted that the family were still tenants but on the matter of being deprived of part of their holding, he had little to say, 'I don't say there has been no diminution of the holding. It may be or it may not be.' The other spokesman for Rogart was John MacKay, a crofter's son born and brought up in Rogart, who was now a well known railway contractor and who spoke with dukes as easily as he did with crofters. He did not think any written evidence could be produced now but he had no doubt that some reward in connection with the land was promised to recruits and in holding that opinion he was not alone, he said, 'His Grace of Sutherland admitted that to me last night.'

No security

The Commission discovered new cases of crofters suffering through having no security of tenure. Alexander Ross aged 63 said he had lived at Rielonie of Culrain on the Novar estate until 1882. Well known as 'The Bard', he told his story in Gaelic and Sheriff Nicolson translated:

'My rent was £8 and I kept two cows and a heifer and a mare and a foal. I gave no offence to the proprietor except that I was not present at the time of the paying of the rent, and was a little behind with it afterwards. As soon as I was able I paid the rent, all except £2, and I would have paid that too, if they had only given me time.

'I was removed a year from Whitsunday last. They knocked down the house, and we were two nights obliged to live on the hillside. I then got a house from a tenant of Mr MacKay at Achnahannet. Now there isn't much work to be had.

'Yes, I've often written Gaelic verses and poetry. I never wrote a satire against anybody but I may have said some sharp things when I told the people the truth that people didn't like!'

The factor denied that the Bard had been put out for anything he'd written but because he wouldn't cultivate his croft. Bards might be uncommon and worth preserving, he said, but they were not prepared to have this one back.

James Sutherland of Spinningdale told how he lost his land when an estate manager, the factor's brother-in-law, gave it to someone else when James had nine months of the year he'd paid rent for still to run:

'This man that got my place, came with his cows to take possession of a bit of foggage (pasture) that I had, and he took the land. He came when I was threshing barley; but I took the law in my right hand and the flail in my left hand, and I went and gave him a good thrashing, himself and his cows, and he went home with his head bleeding, and he went for a policeman and I got fourteen days in prison.

'I have no land now, not an inch, only paying a rent of £1 for the house and keeping it in thatch myself'.

Good and bad for crofters

Glenurquhart was exceptional in being a fertile glen with a good number of smallholdings, where the people were acknowledged to be comfortable and happy. Among those who praised their condition was an Inverness town councillor, Charles MacKay who wanted to see holdings like these in many different parts of the Highlands. Nearer to Inverness on the Leachkin above the Caledonian Canal, he said wasteland of sixty years ago had been transformed into productive holdings by some hardworking people. Money payments for reclaiming land and low rents in the early years had been incentives to them to push on with improvement. The result, in Fraser MacKintosh's eyes, was a joy to see — 'The Leachkin, as a matter of picturesqueness, is a very pretty object as lotted out, particularly at harvest time.'

East coast crofters elsewhere came to explain how they had been cleared off fertile low ground to make room for large farms and moved to barren higher ground and stripped of their common grazing. This happened on the Heights of Strathpeffer where, according to Donald MacDonald of Inchvannie, there were forty-eight crofters suffering now from high rents and game, such as deer, mountain hares and even rabbits which they did not dare destroy without running the risk of removal. The same thing happened on the Black Isle on the Findon estate. John Fowler of Braefindon claimed twenty-four families had created new crofts for themselves, by bringing about ten acres each of new ground into cultivation up the slopes of the Millbuie. They had built their own houses at their own expense and had received no compensation for the improvements they had made. He had no complaint about rabbits — 'It is such a poor place up at Millbuie that rabbits will not live on it!'

Ultimately old Colin Chisholm, a retired customs officer, urged the Royal Commission to consider the vast areas of the Highlands like his native Glencannich and neighbouring Strathglass, where many crofters once lived and which used to produce numbers of soldiers and men of the church, but were now empty glens.

'In Strathglass,' he declared, 'from one end to the other, you will not find one crofter at all, they cleared them out so thoroughly.'

'We never expected such a man as Mr Winans (William Louis Winans, an American millionaire reputed to hold the stalking rights in nearly a quarter of a million acres of deer forest). As long as you leave the laws of the land as they are, and the greed of landlords as it now is, you may have plenty of Americans, Frenchmen, Russians, and any other men.

'I am certainly not against deer stalking, but ach! I don't like his butchering style of killing game at all — gathering the poor animals together and driving them before the muzzles of the guns. He doesn't stalk them. You might as well send an elephant to stalk them'.

It was not only in deer forests that crofters were becoming thin on the ground because in three days of meetings in Inverness almost no crofters appeared at all. Instead the Commissioners heard long detailed statements being read by ministers and land law reformers, landlords, farmers and factors. Some farmers like Thomas Purves from Strathnaver, and factors like James Mollison at Dochfour whose responsibilities included Glenelg in the west, welcomed the opportunity to challenge statements crofters had made there months before and to have their own say about the crofters knowing that none of them were in the audience at Inverness. 'Long and exhaustive' was a Commissioner's public comment on one of the statements, but probably he was only being polite. Although not lively, several of the submissions were useful to the Commission in their enquiry.

One witness at Inverness was Alexander MacKenzie author of *The Highland Clearances*. He had toured the Highlands before the Commissioners arrived, encouraging the people to speak out, and had been present at a good number of their meetings. He advocated the break-up of deer forests and big farms to form smallholdings of varying size, which crofters would hold on permanent tenure, and looked for a Government scheme to help them to become owners of their land if they wished. He admitted that he had been critical when the names of the Commissioners had been announced but having seen how the Royal Commission had carried out its task, he had changed his mind.

'I have no hesitation' he said, 'in saying that everybody is getting ample justice and fair play in the inquiry,' which in his view was 'the most important event for the Highlanders since the battle of Culloden'.

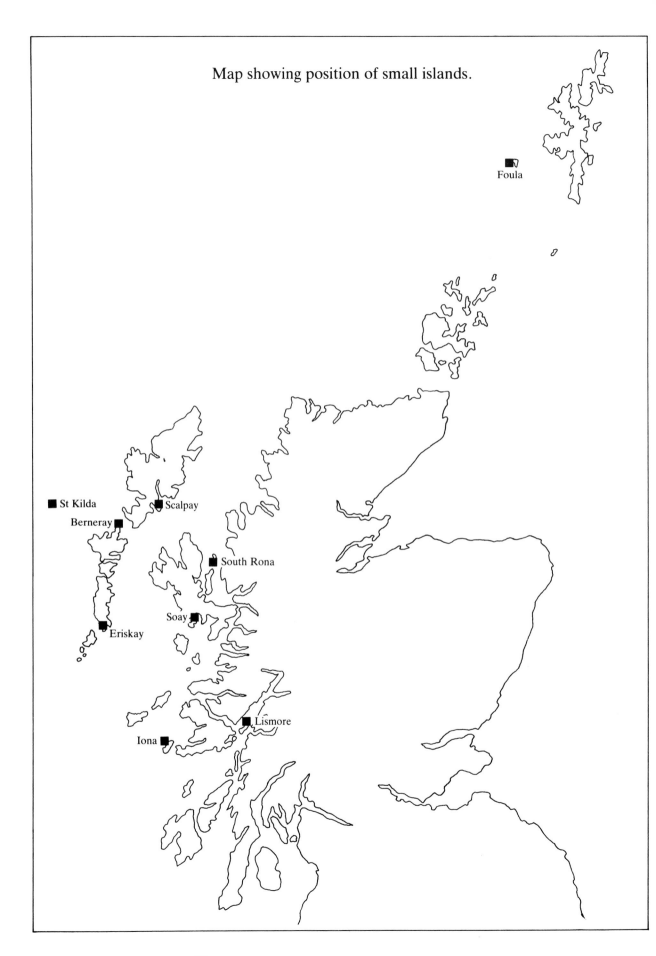

Map showing position of small islands.

People on Small Islands

Visitors on holiday today are often attracted by the idea of spending the rest of their lives on a small island. Most small islands, of course, are emptier now and the contrast between them and large cities is much greater; but island life appeals for many reasons — its peace and quiet, the living in tune with nature, the natural environment for children to grow up in, the satisfaction work gives when providing for one's own simple needs, combined with the neighbourliness and the sense of community with other people sharing the same bit of land and cut off from the rest of the world by water.

On their travels, the Commissioners were to hear from many crofters and others what life was like on a small island a century ago, starting with South Rona north of Raasay.

South Rona

George Grant MacKay of Glengloy (page 17), well known as an agricultural improver, told them he had bought the island in 1872 and discovered to his astonishment that he had on his hands an extreme example of runrig, which he described:

'The arable land was only long straggling strips and patches among the rocks. If there were ten men in a township and only one acre in a piece of ground, the top of it would be divided into ten pieces, and the middle of it into ten pieces, and the bottom into ten pieces, so that an acre would be divided into thirty pieces in all. The consequence was that in the whole island there was not a piece of land bigger than an ordinary room. And to crown the absurdity of the whole thing, every man changed his lot every year, so that the land a man had this year he would not have again for ten years.'

MacKay's solution had been simple and immediate. He divided the land among them, gave every man his own lot in one place and raised his rent by £1 but, he discovered, 'they abused me for what I did' and it did not solve the problem — too many people with too little land. John Nicolson jun., who was 36, was a crofter-fisherman in South Rona where, on the factor's admission, he had only 1¼ acres on which to try to feed a family of six:

'Should I be here from sunrise to sunset I could not fully disclose the poverty of Rona. It is a place in which no man need expect to make his living. We are working on sea and land, both summer and winter and spring — every quarter of the year — and after that we have only poverty. My skiff is my cart, the wives and the children are the horses, and there is truth in that, because it is the work of horses that they perform. The creel is on their back continually.

'I myself remember the township in which I am being in possession of one man. Then four had it. Now eight have it — I mean eight families, fifty people. (In 1971, there were three people in Rona.) That one man was paying £17,19s. of rent, and now the rent is £25. Two of the families came from Kyle Rona on Raasay, and the rest was their own increase. No one can make a living on Rona, crowded upon each other at present. I am willing to move to the mainland. I would like a place in the land of my birth but I have no mind to go abroad.

'We have gone to the east coast fishing with our bags to sell ourselves there to the highest bidder. But the fishing is a lottery, one year successful and another time not. That happened to me often. I would not want a big boat like those on the east coast given to me on Rona. If I was to be a fisherman I would be a fisherman. If I was to be a crofter I would be a crofter. It would simply be spoiling both — we are not in a good fishing place at all.

'I am thinking now that if a man could get in a good place a bit of ground, and get stock upon it at one time, and get the ground at a reasonable rent, it would be better for him than any fishing I have ever seen'.

Soay

Alexander MacCaskill, a cottar and boatman, was no more cheerful about Soay, a little island south of the Cuillins in Skye.

'My grandfather', he said, 'went to the army — at least he was forced to go — and his bones are bleaching on a West Indian island and now his grandson (myself) was evicted to a rock or island that is not fit to be inhabited. In the time of the last proprietor there were two crofts; now there are twenty-three families, about a hundred people on the island. We pay £3 for a croft and the grazing of a cow, and at first we were to have four milk goats, and a cow, and ten sheep and a horse, but we lost the grazing for the sheep and no horse can stand upon it. Some crofts are bogs and rocks, heather and fern, that is all. There are portions of it where, if I were to throw a pail of sea-ware off my back, you would suppose you were standing at the foot of Mount Etna — it would shake as long as there was bog to shake!

'No drainage has been done: Baron Rothschild's money wouldn't drain it. The only thing to do is to remove the inhabitants out of the island altogether. (This happened in 1953 but it has people living on it again.)

'We live by fishing. Every cent we get is by fishing. I just keep body and soul together by it, and keep my aged parents out of the poorhouse. It is not a good station for ling but it is for herring.

'There is an old church over at the island, which was destroyed. We took a piece of the old pulpit and one or two pews. The proprietor belonged to the Established Church and he sent us to Portree. I went there, lost two days and was sent to Edinburgh, and the authorities there were so kind to us that we were not out of lodgings till we came home. I mean we were in the Calton Jail.

'We haven't a minister, we haven't seen one these five months back. The nearest church is the parish church in Bracadale. As you say, we'd need balloons to go to church! Or give us the *Lively* and we will go'.

Eriskay

Were things better in the Outer Isles? Another MacCaskill, John, spoke for the people of Eriskay, between South Uist and Barra:

'There are eighty-four paying rent in Eriskay, and about a dozen families who pay no rent, chiefly paupers. Three occupied it formerly. There are three times the number on the island than should be on it. The others came about thirty-five years ago from Uist. They were sent across to the island. The population is between 400 and 500 (now 200).

'The men always go to the east coast fishing. They mostly return home next winter, except a few young men who go abroad in ships. I was often abroad. I was round the coast of Scotland generally, and in England,

Eriskay from the west.

Ireland and America as a sailor but if I had means of satisfactorily keeping the place at home, there is no place where I would be so healthy and happy as in Eriskay.

'Young women go south to work. Some of them remain away and some return but I don't know of any family who have left our place at all.

'The people are Roman Catholics, except two or three families, and we have a Catholic Church. We also have a public school. Almost all the population, except the young children who are at school, cannot read and write. A few about my own time of life (he was 38) got a little education, but very few. The children attend the school regularly: they have to go. The people complain of the rates for the school, 8d. in the pound — 4d. on the landlord, 4d. on the tenant, but we know that it is a good pennyworth'.

Berneray

Malcolm MacLeod, the 42-year-old cottar who composed the account of his island north of North Uist for the Royal Commission, wrote it in Gaelic. This was very unusual. Nearly all the written evidence submitted to the Commission was in English: 549 letters in English had been received — over one-third of the incoming mail — before the first letter appeared in Gaelic. He had learned to write Gaelic at home, he said, he never learned it at school. 72 people had been present at the meeting in Berneray and agreed Malcolm's statement was true.

'The population of the island is 454, having increased during the last ten years by 72. The island is about 3 miles long by 2 broad. A native of North Uist (Mr John MacDonald of Newton whom we have met) rents much more than half of it, in the farm of Borve. His end of the island is the better soil today whatever. He has both cattle and sheep on it but there is not much of it under crop this year. There is a stone dyke on the east side between the crofters and Mr MacDonald. He has about thirteen cottars on his farm besides his own servants. On our portion of the island there are sixty-five families, twenty tenants, ten with half lots, and thirty-five cottars without a foot of land.

'We need to reduce rents to the figure in my grandfather's time before kelp nearly doubled it. Our holdings are so small and bad that we cannot live upon them. We cannot leave a portion untilled to give it a rest, as is necessary. Some parts are so rocky we must carry soil on our backs before we can sow seed in it, and after all our exertions there are twenty crofters on the island who have not ground grain for a twelve-month back. We have to get our meal from Glasgow. If it were not for the manufacture of home tweeds by the women, we could not live at all.

'When families grow up and marry and have families, they have no room on their father's land to make a livelihood and so they must seek it on the sea. Many of them go lobster-fishing. In former times — I am ashamed to tell you how some of the people lived — they lived on shell-fish, limpets. Those who had boats went out to the rocks twice a day when the ebb occurred at forenoon and evening. Now we fish lobsters but from want of nets we cannot go to fish herrings. Every year we think we can fish out of the Atlantic what will buy nets for us, but we have our wages pledged for food before the fishing begins.

'Mr John MacDonald, Newton, North Uist who rents Borve now is very kind to us. He gives the cottars potato ground in return for work, whatever work is to be done on the farm. I am not sure what it comes to: it used to be ground for a barrel of potatoes for four days' work. The payment is never in money'.

St Kilda

About mid-day on Saturday, 2nd June, the *Lively* arrived off St Kilda after a 60-mile journey. Wild stormy weather had made it uncertain when they would depart from West Loch Tarbert, and nobody on the island knew they were coming. The *Lively* was the first ship to bring strangers to St Kilda that year and the people, 77 in number, were in some fear of catching colds from the visitors or diseases like measles or smallpox.

Hurriedly the little church was made ready for a meeting. It had whitewashed walls and a floor of bare earth inside. About twenty well-built men sat on wooden forms as the minister, John MacKay, opened the proceedings with prayer. Donald Macdonald, a 37-year old crofter-

The church on St Kilda.

fisherman who was described in *The Scotsman* as 'a very manly fellow', spoke for the islanders. First he explained about their rents in an island which seldom used money.

'We do not pay in money but with all the produce which the island gives — feathers, and oil, and cloth, and also with cattle. The proprietor gives us 5s. a stone for the grey feathers, and 6s. a stone for the black feathers, puffin feathers, which are finer. For the fulmar oil he pays us 1s. a pint and 3s. a *Scotch ell* (37 inches, less than a metre) for our cloth. We never got such good prices before for our cattle as under the present factor. We get £2,10s. and we have got £3 for a stirk from him.

'The island would not keep us in meal any time: we get it from the mainland. Some families get eight to twelve bolls in the year. It is paid for in the produce of the island in the same way as the rent. Last summer we got a few bolls by steamer and we sold a little cloth to the steamer at prices which were a little better.

'We would like a pier for purposes of fishing. If you saw some of the days when we have to land here, you would understand then what need we have of it. Only two boats go out to fish now: we have fallen off in able-bodied men. We catch ling and some cod. I know that the herring comes here, sometimes into this loch. There were Lewis men fishing here three years ago. We do not fish for herring because we have no herring nets.

'Twenty years ago we used to pay £1 for the rocks on which we caught the birds but when complaint was made, the laird took £1 off the rocks and put it on us for the island of Boreray, which previously cost us 5s. We catch the birds (fulmars) to get the oil at the beginning of summer. We catch the young ones with our hands before they are able to fly off their nests. We catch the old birds with the rod and snare. We go down the rocks on a rope, and place the snare over the bird's head, and catch it by the neck. I cannot give a guess how many birds are caught here annually, probably thousands but I cannot say. One day I remember we were snaring the birds on Boreray when we caught at least 1000. There were twenty men of us, but I never saw or heard of so many being caught again'.

The St Kilda people sharing out the fulmars in 1886, Donald MacDonald standing barefoot third from the left and Mrs MacDonald on the extreme right.

The St Kilda men on the cliffs of Boreray 1896.

Afterwards, four of the men demonstrated how they caught the birds. One of them, Donald Gillies with a rope round his waist, lowered himself hand over hand on another rope to a green ledge 200 feet down and caught three birds on the nest with a wand with a slip-knot snare.

Then the Commissioners went to look at the houses. They saw that they were well built in a row or street, and better roofed than many in the Highlands. They found that the women had dressed up in their homespun dresses with gay cotton kerchiefs fastened with copper or bone pins and were busy knitting outside. Going inside they saw the loom, the carding implements and the spinning wheels standing among heaps of raw wool. The walls and the rafters were brown with smoke, and bladders full of the strong-smelling oil from the fulmars were hanging over the fireplace. Some of the older girls 'with experience of Glasgow', the *Scotsman* correspondent said, shocked him by expecting the visitors to pay. (One wonders what he would have thought of the owners of stately homes who open them to the public today!) The Commissioners, however, had come well armed and gave people presents of shawls, coloured handkerchiefs, tea, tobacco and sweets.

Scalpay, Harris

John MacDiarmid who had been a crofter and a fisherman in his day was now 88. When *The Graphic*'s artist saw him he was immediately impressed by John's tawny hair and his instant flow of language as he told the Commissioners in the Free Church in Tarbert about the people in his island to the east:

'They are very poor and very crowded. The whole of the population — crofters and cottars — have to pursue the fishing, chiefly lobster-fishing, and they have to be out summer, spring and winter, at least eleven months of the year. They have often to go from home, and live in bothies. Then everybody that can go to the east coast fishing goes there — to Wick. On their return, they take to the home fishing, some to the long line fishing, and others at the fall of the year to lobster-fishing. They have fished their own shore clean and have to pursue the lobster-fishing at a distance, all the way to Lochmaddy.

'First there were twenty families in the island, then a second twenty were sent in. The families of the original settlers were growing up and having families of their own, and now there are close on a hundred families in the place. Their families are sharing their own little bits of land with them'.

The factor's Return showed that no other family was as crowded as his own, the MacDiarmids. It had nine branches, living in nine separate houses — 51 people altogether — all on one croft so small that its rent was only £2,5s. a year, and with only two cows, two calves and seven sheep between the lot of them.

'There seemed to be no way they could make a living out of it at all but a native of the place was able through Providence to set up a curing establishment and he provided for the people necessities, and took from them the fish they caught. He has kept them going for the last twenty-eight years. He provided them with boats and nets to fish the Minch — the early herring fishing between here and Skye — before they went to the east coast fishing. But for the last two years, this early fishing has failed completely and it is quite easy for you to understand that times must be hard on a little island with 500 souls on the surface of it.'

The Graphic commended the Commissioners for the patience they showed with old men like John who appeared before them and generally started their evidence with the Battle of Waterloo, but who would not want to listen when they have the chance to hear him tell the story of a clearance as dramatically as this?

'I will tell you how Rodel was cleared. Ther were 150 hearths in Rodel. Forty of these paid rent. When young MacLeod came home with his newly-married wife to Rodel he went away to show his wife the place and twenty of the women of Rodel came and met them and danced a reel before them, so glad were they to see them. By the time the year was out — twelve months from that day, these twenty women were weeping and wailing; their houses being unroofed and their fires quenched by the orders of the estate. I could not say who was to blame, but before the year was out 150 fires were quenched. Some of the more capable of these tenants were sent to Berneray, and others were crowded into the Bays on the east side of Harris — small places that kept three families in comfort where now there are eight. Some of the cottars that were among these 150 were for a whole twelve months in the shielings before they were able to provide themselves with permanent residences. Others of them got, through the favour of Mrs Campbell of Strond, the site of a house upon the sea-shore upon places reclaimed by themselves'.

Foula

From St Magnus Bay in Shetland the Commissioners enjoyed a three hour sail south-west to Foula under a bright sun. Seeing the *North Star* coming, some of the fishermen, still with their lines and a good catch of ling and cod on board, rowed out to meet them. The men rowed strongly and in unison. With their hair and beards long, and wearing dark woollen blouses, they appeared, to the *Scotsman* correspondent at least, to have the look of pirates. Landing on the east side at Ham which smelt of fish and where rows of fish were drying in the sun, they found Foula to be an island rich in wild flowers, buttercup, yellow iris and red campion. When the children appeared, twenty-five in number, they were rewarded with sweets: for them too, this would be a day to remember.

There were only 275 people in the island, living on 40 crofts, sixteen miles from the mainland. (In 1983, the number of people in Foula was down to 45). Originally Foula's two delegates were to be heard at Lerwick and a subscription was raised on the island to pay their expenses, but since then the *Lively* had sunk. This time the school was prepared for the meeting but, with the weather so fine, it seemed better to stay out in the open air. Robert Gear who was the catechist as well as a crofter, told them about their work on the land:

'Each of us has three or four acres of arable land and two or three cows — small ones. I think three cows is the average besides young ones. The average number of sheep may be perhaps half a dozen. Some have fifty or sixty, and others none at all. We have no horses. The proprietor has a few horses on the island but none of the crofters is allowed to keep them. Horses would be of use to us to carry home turf. Our peats are abundant but in some parts of the island they have to come here for them. Both men and women carry the peats, but mostly it is the men. All the hard work is not put on the women. We might also use horses for ploughing. In Shetland they do all the turning of the soil with the spade and it is the same here.

'No crop grows well here. The potatoes are of poor quality. The crops are liable to be destroyed by the sea and by violent gales. The best return of oats we can get in a good year is, I suppose, three or four-fold. We don't grow any other crop but for bere.

'The wool is black-faced principally now. The native breed is practically out; they have been crossed with black-faced. We have a bad quality of wool. The women all knit out of the local wool. They make small shawls and stockings — of the coarse kind; none of the fine shawls. They are taken from them by Messrs Garriock, who have the shop. Sometimes if the men go out with their boats for fishing, the women may go too and take what they have ready to the mainland'.

Others joined in as the proceedings became more of a conversation than a formal enquiry. They agreed that they could not live off their crofts alone. James Gray who was 50 recalled only one year in the last twenty-six when he 'could bread his family without buying meal'. They disagreed about how much they could make from fishing, taking one year with another. James Gray said '£4 to £6. I never run above £10'. Robert Paterson, a 38-year-old crofter and fisherman, claimed he had once had £20 in a year, but that was 'when I was a young fisherman and had health at the time'. He agreed with Professor MacKinnon that 'there is nothing here but the point of the hook to turn to'.

'They have to fish or leave the place', he said. 'A good many young men have gone, there are some in Australia and New Zealand. They go to sail in ships, and to the diggings and to farming and so on.

'For catching ling off Foula this year we get 8s.6d. a cwt., 5s. to 7s. for cod and 5s. for tusk. The cod livers are our property. They are thrown into a barrel and taken home by us for light or sale. We use cods' heads for food, and tusks' and lings' too. For ordinary bait when there are no herring, we use small cod, turbot and halibut, and limpet for the hand lines. I have never gone to the herring fishing. We have never gone in for it, but two crews are trying it this year'.

John Henry, another crofter-fisher the same age as Robert Paterson, spoke up on food and the cost of living:

'We are very apt to grumble that the things in Mr Garriock's shop are too dear. We are paying 5s.11d. for a pound of English tobacco and we think that rather dear. That is for twist, and we get no tea here below 8d. per quarter of a pound. For hard sugar we pay 6d. a pound for soft 4½d. I agree we consume a lot of tea and sugar, more than we are fit to purchase.

'We grumble a lot about the price of our eggs. We eat as few as we can: we have to give them in to pay for meal. We only get 4d. to 6d. per dozen

Inside a Foula house in 1902, fishing lines, clothes and fish hanging above the peat fire.

for them at the shop. The shopkeeper says the shells are thin and the eggs liable to break.

'Milk is scarce in winter, when we give the children a little sugar and water instead. Ordinarily we eat porridge very much the same as our fathers did. For breakfast in winter we have bread and milk when we have it, and sometimes a little black bread and a cup of tea. Fish and potatoes for dinner, but they are not potatoes: you could wring the water out of them'.

Sheriff Nicolson made them laugh by saying that fish and potatoes seemed to have made them as big and strong men as they had seen anywhere. They admitted that most of them were very healthy, and perhaps none the worse of living on an island without a doctor.

When this extraordinary meeting — a landmark in the island's history — was over, the Commissioners walked to the top of the high cliffs to enjoy the view, then the islanders went with them down to the shore to see them off. Clearly, these were people who might be poor but were obviously attached to their island and pleased to have been visited.

The Foula men with their boat.

Iona

Malcolm Ferguson, a 46-year-old crofter from East End, Iona travelled to
Glasgow to speak for the island, which pleased the Commissioners
because storms had prevented them from visiting it themselves. He began
by pointing out the effects on the islanders of the loss of their right to cut
peats over on the Ross of Mull:

'By having the peat moss they were saving the price of coals. They
would require £5 or more for coals in the year. They were saving that by
carting and ferrying peats with their own boats, when there was no other
employment that they (the woman on page 87) could be at.

'There are eight cottars in the township each paying rent of £1 a year
for houses they built themselves and 10s. for an eighth of an acre as a
kailyard. I can't tell you if they are black houses or white houses. They are
whitewashed anyhow! The Duke (of Argyll) was giving them lime at times
to whitewash them. The cottars support themselves by fishing and
working here and there. Some of them are tradesmen, but not all.

'I pay £14,18s. rent for my croft and I'm allowed to keep eight cows
and a horse or their equivalent in sheep. Five sheep are the equivalent of

a cow on Iona. I know from my own knowledge and experience that people have to borrow to pay the rent. For the last fourteen or fifteen years I did not put a shoe on my foot, a shirt on my back or a bonnet on my head, with any profit I derived from the croft.

'Compared with twenty years ago, the Cathedral (as the Abbey was often called them) is now an object of great beauty, cleaned out and repaired at the expense of the Duke of Argyll. Everyone that was working there was paid: it was regular paid work. It is now under the charge of a native of Iona (John MacDonald).

'If we were able to build very nice cottages in Iona, we would be able to take the rent out of the place, by keeping lodgers in the summer time. Of late years, the place has been becoming a favourite resort for summer visitors. Very few stay at the hotel; but the other class of people, that are not in such a high position as to stay in the hotel, are taking up a good many houses in the island. They prefer living in private cottages'.

Women gathering seaweed beside the Abbey on Iona.

Lismore

The Royal Commission held its last meeting of the summer in the Baptist Church at Bachuil in Lismore. This green island in Loch Linnhe is nearly ten miles long and two miles wide. James Wilson, the school teacher at Baligarve who was also the registrar, told the Commission that the population in the island was falling, down to 750 in 1871, and down again to 637 in 1881. The reason, he thought, was the small number of marriages, only about two a year, because people either could not afford or could not find a place to bring up a family. Hugh Carmichael of Port Ramsay agreed, saying some had 'grown old in the condition of bachelors and had not been able to make a home for themselves'. Alexander Buchanan of Killean, who said to Sheriff Nicolson, 'I don't know if you are one or not', agreed and added about himself, 'I live in lodgings because I didn't marry. It's my own fault'. He recalled the old parish minister saying that in his early days in 1821, the population in the island had been much higher, 1650 in all.

From John Fraser Sim of Oban, the factor, they learned that the people of Lismore were a people by themselves:

'On Rev Mr Fell's property, I draw rent from 59 people, and 57 are aborigines of the place. They have their own habits, customs and sympathies. They are clannish when they get among strangers; they fight a good deal among themselves; they have their own patron Saint (St

Moluag); altogether the island is an island by itself'.

Hugh Carmichael was one of 16 crofters at Port Ramsay who each had two acres of arable only and pasture in common. People needed extra help, he said.

'I had a small vessel, a smack and went about with it. My sons go now, they are working away in it there. The trade is in lime and stone and slate and that — all the local traffic. The Oban railway (opened in 1880) has spoiled the lime traffic for us. My smack, and many others, has been quite idle for the last two months'.

The people of Port Ramsay were not crofters in the ordinary sense, the factor said:

'Five of them own vessels. One of them carries 65 tons, another 70, another 30 and two others 20. There is a boat-builder here (old Duncan MacDonald), a shopkeeper, a retired farmer, a shoemaker, four labourers only, and a widow woman'.

MacIntyre's lime quarries were the best source of regular work at a wage of 18s. to £1 a week. Usually there were 12 to 16 men there and more in springtime. Dugald Buchanan had worked there since he lost his croft 18 years ago:

'If Mr MacIntyre hadn't given me work, I might have starved altogether. We work in the quarry at all seasons, during the frost in winter too if it is dry frost but not if it is slippery'.

Hugh Cameron, another smack-owner in the lime trade to the islands thought Mr MacIntyre was 'the person upon whom the whole island relies, especially the poor and working class', and agreed that if he had the land, the poor would be better off.

Everyone was convinced the soil was very good in Lismore and its potato crops, in particular, were excellent. The cattle were nearly all Highland cattle but the breed had been much improved. One crofter, Connell Connel, who was 77, admitted that his rent £18,19s. had not been raised since the first rent he paid twenty-four years ago, but he maintained it had gone up in his father's time. He didn't know how much his father used to pay, he said, but the factor soon told him:

'In 1852 his father's rent was, in money £14. He also supplied 80 eggs, 4 fowls, 4 chickens, 1 pint of seal oil, 4 hanks of *lint* (yarn spun from flax), 5s. for *wrack* (seaweed), 1s.3d. for *sids* (inner husks of oats with bits of meal sticking to them), 5 bolls of meal, making £5,14s.11d.: total £19,14s.11d.!'

Since Lismore had no peats now, the cost of burning imported coal, £5, or £6 a year, was old Connell's main complaint.

He offered the Commission a new definition of fair rent, 'If the price of the coals were deducted from the rent, I would be content'.

Lismore had had no public house for the last seven or eight years: thirty years ago it had had five! Dugald MacIntyre, a farmer, did not think the want of a public house was an inconvenience to strangers, who might prefer a temperance hotel. 'There was no policeman living on the island, and little need for one', he said, 'now that the public house was done away with'.

'But you are not an impartial judge', Sheriff Nicolson reminded him, 'I see you have the Blue Ribbon' (showing that he was a Total Abstainer)!

Going home

Leaving Lismore, three of the Commissioners Lord Napier, Sir Kenneth Mackenzie and Fraser MacKintosh made for Fort William to catch the daily steamer along the Caledonian Canal to Inverness and two of them went home from there by train — two modes of transport which were not available to people who spent their lives in small islands.

Women's Work and Why

'A woman's work is never done' — the Commissioners were about to discover just how true this was for women living on a croft. As long as crofting was a subsistence economy in which each family had to try to provide for its own simple needs — its food, a roof over their heads, their clothes — by their own efforts, husband and wife learned to work together and to share the work out between them.

In and around the home

They accepted a fairly traditional division of labour, each doing what he or she was better at. For example he, having greater strength, gathered the stones and built the house but inside, she was the mistress — she cooked, she baked, she looked after the children. Being more deft with her hands, she spun on her spinning-wheel the wool from their own sheep into homespun yarn, which means what it says, 'wool spun in the home'. This was the kind of work she could turn to in any spare moment

Woman on Scalpay, Harris, carding wool on the right, spinning on the left.

she had — 'when the women get something of ease from the working of the land', was how a North Lewis weaver put it. In the Western Isles and more distant St Kilda, it was commonly the woman who was the weaver whereas in Unst in Shetland, weaving had normally been a male occupation. She worked on a hand loom and might weave blankets, or cloth for making up into clothes for the family, John MacDonald, part crofter, part tailor of Roshkill, near Dunvegan in Skye, remembered when he was a boy women weaving their webs of cloth, twenty to twenty seven yards long, in their own homes. He used to make his living going round working in people's houses, and making the clothes each member of the family needed. But now things had changed. Little cloth was being woven in the district now, or indeed in the whole of Skye, because so many crofters had lost the pasture for their sheep, while their wives bought factory-made cloth and made it into clothes themselves, leaving less work for the tailor to do. Talking about the homespun cloth made out of their own wool in the old days, Murdo MacLeod of Digg in the north of Skye reckoned it cost very little, only about 1s.6d. a yard to make and explained why:

Weaving on Skye early this century.

'Our own women did the spinning and the dyeing. It was the work of the women which was making it so cheap. The women were getting the dye stuffs off the rocks. They could make six or seven different colours, or perhaps nine or ten. We can dye with tea, peat soot, lichens, heather tops, and bark of willow, but we don't use tea in making dye — it is too scarce a commodity' (actually the only one for which they had to pay money).

Many women still spun in the 1880s, using wool they bought from neighbouring farmers or which their husbands brought home after working in the south. Then in the evenings, they would sit knitting socks or stockings, and pass on the skill to their children. Another task which fell to the woman as an extension of her work in the home was milking, probably because the cows were under the same roof in winter in the Outer Isles, and she was usually at home. Turning a *quern,* a hand-mill consisting of two round stones for grinding grain to separate the meal for the family to eat, was usually a woman's work; but although querns were still to be seen all over the islands, they were not often in use. Families were buying oatmeal, which had already been ground, instead of growing their own grain. It was the woman too who kept the hens and sold the eggs but, declared John MacKay a Skye crofter, 'The women get the money; the men take nothing to do with the likes of that'.

Compulsory labour

Before ordinary people in the Highlands were in the habit of handling money, they paid rent for their land in *service*, doing so many days' labour on their superior's land or in *kind*, giving him so much produce from their own land. Women gave service as well as men and, although paying rents in money had been the rule for a good many years, the Royal Commission discovered in 1883 cases of cottars' families still being bound to work for the farmer on whose farm they lived. In Skye for example, Alexander Cameron, a cottar of Cuilmore reported that he was required to provide a maid servant for the sheep farm of Drynoch for fifty days a year at a wage of only 6d. or 8d. a day. His sister did the work until she married, in spite of the wage being so low that it did not even keep her in food. When he failed to supply another woman to take her place — he had no one in his family — he received a summons to the sheriff court and was threatened with eviction, not because the farmer really wanted to turn him out, the factor said, but as an example to encourage the other cottars to keep on supplying maid servants to do 'woman's work' on the farm. He was not evicted in the end, but his rent was raised by £1 a year to make up to the farmer for the loss of a woman's labour.

On the land

Cultivating the land was man's work but women were expected to help. Probably when crofts were bigger and the land was better, more crofters had horses and there was less fieldwork for women to do; but poverty increased the burden on women, and on children too, and men were often ashamed of the work they had to get women to do. For example, in reply to Cameron of Lochiel, William MacLure of Glen Bernisdale in Skye agreed that his croft needed something better than himself with a caschrom, a foot plough, to cultivate it, but the crofters had no horses:

'We must take a horse's work out of a woman, we get them to harrow (pull a wooden frame with pointed teeth to break up the soil or cover the seed) — while slavery is done away with in other countries, it is likely to continue here'.

The Commissioners were to hear the same message from an old mason at Dunvegan a week later — 'We had no horses, our women had to do it, dragging the harrows with a rope about their shoulders, helping the men with forks and spades in digging the ground'. They heard it again in Raasay the week after that — 'The wives and children are the horses, the creel is on their back continually'.

Carrying things

They made their own creels, wickerwood baskets, for carrying loads on their backs, and they made them in different sizes to suit the strength of those who had to carry them. Not having barrows, or carts, or ponies which, with panniers like creels on each side, could carry as much as two women, people with creels became their own beasts of burden. They carried seaweed from the shore to manure their land, a long way in many places and a considerable number of times because soils which were peaty or exhausted needed a great deal if they were to yield a crop at all. Planting potatoes in spring, as the picture on page x shows, the man made the drill with the caschrom or spade, the woman spread the seaweed along it and put in the seed. Then in the autumn, the whole family would be involved in gathering the crop, and carrying it home on their backs.

Peats were the other important load which people commonly carried in creels. Usually the men cut the peats before going off to summer jobs and

Shetland women knitting as they carry peats.

Mary MacPherson spinning with distaff and spindle on the way to the peats, about 1820.

the women and children set them up to dry. In some places, the distance from the peat bank to the croft was several miles, and if the photographs taken at the time are any guide, the peat-carriers in this, a very labour-intensive form of transport, were usually women. The reasons given for carrying peats this way include the lack of roads, or where roads did exist, the cost of hiring a cart, the availability of the women and girls anyway when they had no paid employment to prevent them, and the need to get a year's supply home somehow. Shetland women carrying peats were more productive. John Anderson, a merchant at Hillswick said they used to spin while carrying peats and walking. (This can only have been with the distaff and spindle.) Many photographs show other women busy knitting as they walked. Peat banks for the Iona crofters were on the Ross of Mull and it was the women who went across in boats to cut the peats. They used to leave at three or four o'clock in the morning, taking their dinner with them, and would not be home in Iona until nine o'clock at night. Later when they had their potatoes set up, they would cross again to Mull to cart their peats down to the shore and ferry them home by boat. It was not the case everywhere, however, that so much of the peat-work was done by women. To take two examples from Shetland, it was the fishermen of Papa Stour who complained of the twenty-four days a year they lost, having to go to Papa Little nine miles away for peats when they could have been fishing; and in Foula, Robert Gear the catechist said, 'Both men and women carry the peats, but mostly the men — we do not put all the hard work on the women here'.

The Commissioners discovered from Angus Matheson Polson, a Golspie merchant, that fishermen's wives at Embo and Golspie on the east coast of Sutherland endured heavier loads and harsher lives:

'The fisherwomen carry mussel bait in creels (weighing when full about two cwt. each), a distance out and in of about eight miles. They redd (unravel) the lines and also bait them. They dig in the sand with spades — arduous work even for men — for certain kinds of bait. In the coldest days of winter, they are obliged to wade much over knee-deep (and that barefooted) into the chilly brine. They assist in launching and hauling up the boats. They carry the men into and out of the boats, because here they have no harbours. I can hardly say why they carry their husbands ashore on their backs: it is really a sad state of affairs. The men are often very tired, and in going out again, they require to get out to the boats dry'.

At the shielings

If there were a happy time for women and children to look forward to in the crofting year, it was surely the beginning of June when they would drive their sheep and cattle up to the shielings. These were their summer pastures in the hills where they would stay in huts built of stone and turf for about six weeks, and the animals would graze on the fresh pastures around them. This movement of stock up to higher pastures gave the grass nearer home a chance to grow and be fit to feed the animals later in the year. The custom was for the men to go up to repair the huts for them, and then to go away to their summer work such as the herring fishing, leaving the women up there in charge. The Royal Commission heard more in Skye about the grazings the crofters had lost to the sheep farmers and little about shielings, even memories of them long ago. In Harris, Donald Harrison of Geocrab who was 76, told what he remembered about them — the women singing as they were milking the cows, making butter and cheese and spinning in the open air. To spin they would hold the raw wool on a distaff in one hand, draw it out and twist it by turning a spindle with their fingers — a much slower method than the spinning wheel. 'We had pleasant times there', he said, 'we slept on the floor with the heather below us. The women would sing and dance and have tunes'. In Lewis, however, the custom of going up to the shielings was still carried on as John Matheson had told them (page 28) at Barvas but the Barvas women did not make butter and cheese there any more. To the islanders of Great Bernera in Lewis, having shielings on the mainland was especially important. The women went ashore with the cattle about 9th June and stayed there with them the whole summer, without ever going home. Those who could make butter and cheese did so; those who couldn't, had to do without. The men went over to take them food and bring back the milk. To give some idea of the numbers of women and children going to their shieling, Murdo MacDonald who belonged to Tobson township where twenty-five crofting families and twenty cottars lived, reckoned there would be about thirty. They would spend each day 'knitting stockings, making shirts, caps and frocks, and such like work', he said, 'and looking after the cows', and the young people especially liked to keep up the custom of singing together in the evening, needing no instruments to accompany them.

Making things to sell — hosiery and tweed

Unfortunately in the Highlands and Islands, there were almost no enterprises which provided work for women near home in return for pay. Gutting herrings in Barra and Stornoway and places like Mid Yell in Shetland, was the exception, but its season was short. What women could do in some places was to make things for sale. In Shetland, this gave rise to the important knitting industry. Arthur James Hay, a merchant and factor in Lerwick, reckoned that Shetland hosiery, using fine Shetland wool commanded higher prices in 1883 than previously. No machinery was used because there was no water power or steam power in the islands. Women spun all the wool at home on their spinning wheels. Women in the island in Unst were in the habit of knitting shawls especially, as well as some stockings, and on the mainland James R. Sutherland the old minister of Northmavine parish said the women were doing so well from knitting, 'you cannot get them to be servants or anything else'. The

Pegging out fine Shetland shawls to dry near Lerwick in 1890.

women in his parish specialised in knitting underclothing for both women and men, using the pure Shetland wool only, because the customers preferred it and were willing to pay extra to get it. John Anderson, the local merchant and fish-curer, bought the garments the women made, and occasionally sold them wool when their own supply ran out. He believed some of the old women could keep themselves, just by knitting. In Orkney, on the other hand, it was said that women had no chance to earn in this way.

In the islands in the west, one or two members of land-owning families tried to help to find a market for the socks and stockings the women knitted. Miss MacLeod of MacLeod did this in Skye, and Lady Cathcart on her estate on South Uist but her factor complained of having thousands of pairs of socks and stockings he could not sell. A North Uist crofter wished there were someone to buy from their wives who were also good knitters. They sold to the shops and to anybody who was willing to buy. They received 6d. for a pair of socks, which seems a low price when the women were also providing and spinning the wool, and 1s.6d. for a pair of long stockings.

The encouragement of tweed-making in Harris did most to give women the chance to earn by working in their homes. Angus Campbell of Plocrapool reckoned the people of the Bays in Harris could not have made a living without it, having poor land and no sheep. He had a seven ton boat himself and he went to buy wool for them in the Uists and elsewhere, bringing back as much as 500 stones of wool in a year. 'Their wives through the night manufacture it into cloth', he said. He named the Countess Dowager of Dunmore (whose late husband used to own the whole of Harris) and Mrs Captain Thomas as the two who promoted the sale of their cloth far beyond Harris. Roderick MacKenzie, the Free Church minister there since 1868 and Kenneth MacDonald of Scaristavore, the factor for North Harris disagreed about which of them deserved the greater credit. The minister suggested it was Mrs Thomas who started it. Her husband Captain F. W. L. Thomas R.N. had carried

Harris tweed draped round a thatched roof to dry.

Skye women in 1772 at the quern on the left the others 'waulking' or fulling cloth on a corrugated board and singing as they worked.

out surveys of the coasts of the Hebrides and also recorded many of the antiquities of the Islands — and the minister owed his manse to the Thomases, as well as the church where they were meeting that day. The factor, who had lived in Harris for fifty years, would have none of it. 'The Countess Dowager was manufacturing webs of cloth before Mrs Captain Thomas was known in this part of the world', he said. 'It brings in an enormous amount of money. I remember one year paying for her £1235 for webs of cloth alone. They make it on hand-looms; they use blackfaced and Cheviot wool, and dyes grown on the island'. The women were good spinners and weavers and were making Harris famous for its tweed all over Britain and abroad. For himself, he was proud of the coat he was wearing which he said was 'grown on the farm, woven on the farm and made on the farm'.

At the end of their meeting in Tarbert the Commissioners had the opportunity to watch women in the communal process of *waulking* (or fulling) the cloth. Seven women were sitting on each side of a table with a corrugated wooden top and working the cloth with their hands, rolling it and beating it, while keeping time to the tune of an old Gaelic song.

Elsewhere, there were women weavers who made into cloth the yarn their neighbours had spun at home. North Uist had twelve, described in the Return of cottars as 'weaveresses', and on the east side of Skye there were seven or eight weavers still working. The demand was still there, especially among older people. One of them, Murdo MacLeod of Digg had only two or three sheep but he told the Commission, 'I manage in a couple of years to provide myself with a pair of trousers and a pair of stocking off them', but the chances are he got the women to make them.

Work away from home

Girls and single women without ties left the islands to go to paid work in the summer. The Commissioners had met some going down to the boat at Colbost in Skye and James Grant, minister of Kilmuir for the last five years, informed them that a great many young women went into domestic service in the south, and some to farm work in the Lothians. The steamer *St Clair* made this possible for girls from the Northern Isles and the extension of steamer services to three boats a week calling at the Uists and Harris made it possible for their girls to go 'abroad', as they called it, to domestic service as well. Other island girls, having worked at the herring packing at home in Barra or Stornoway, took to following the east coast boats, wherever the fishing might be.

Colbost jetty where the Commission saw Skye girls setting off for summer work in the south.

Working on the mainland for pay, these young women could earn their keep, buy some clothes and have a bit left over to bring home when the season was over. Probably it was they who introduced machine-made woollen cloth to the islands and arrived wearing cotton clothes, which made Donald McPhee, the old mason at Dunvegan deplore the changes taking place in the world with 'each woman imitating the fashions — the godless fashions of France!' Over and over again, however, the Commissioners were to hear how much more important was the money they brought — to help their parents to pay the rent or pay off some of their debt for meal. The understanding that the young had a duty to support their parents in their old age was very real. John Mathieson was a cottar at Achnahannet, about a mile from the Braes, and his case is a good example. He was over 50 and not very well, and his wife, an invalid, was confined to her bed. He had applied for poor relief for her and was refused. The reason? Her children, two unmarried daughters, were to support her, the parochial board said, but they were far away, in Nairn, where they were house-servants, hardly the best-paid of occupations.

Widows and crofts

But what chance did a woman without a grown-up son have of holding on to a croft when her husband died? In Mull they tried to find out at first hand about the removal of Widow MacPhail which had got into the Glasgow papers. Duncan MacLean, a crofter in the same township, Artun Bremanoir in the Ross of Mull, said it was over a year since her husband died. He didn't know how old her eldest son was, probably between fourteen and fifteen. He heard she had sent a petition to the Duke of Argyll's chamberlain asking to stay on in the croft:

'She had a full stock and was able to pay the rent, but she did not get the land. It was given to the inspector of the poor, who is collector of poor rates and clerk to the School Board, and used to be a schoolmaster. The first notice she got was this man going about and telling he had got it. Now she is living in the village of Bunessan and she keeps a little shop'.

The chamberlain, James Wyllie, offered no reason for her removal. 'The Duke uses his own discretion' he said, 'he considers each case separately. He declared Widow MacPhail was pretty well off now from the sale of her stock, but they heard of other cases. Mary MacKinnon or MacColl, for example, whose husband died, John McCormick of Catchean told them, was removed a month later.

'She had a full stock and a son about seventeen or eighteen. She was one of the best crofter farmers in Ross but she was sent to another croft, then to another croft, then to a house without a croft.'

The chamberlain provided the information that there were thirty-six widows with crofts in their own name in Tiree but when he added that there were only three in Mull it sounded as if there was some truth in the current opinion that widows in Mull were likely to be turned out of crofts if their children were under the age of twenty-one.

On the other side of the country at Marrel near Helmsdale, Adam Bannerman, a crofter's son discussing wages, said men's wages ranged from 1s.6d. to 3s. a day for harvesting and smearing while some women were paid '2s. to follow the scythe.' Reaffirming that some men were paid only 1s.6d., and that some women earned more, he maintained that some of the women were better workers than the men. It is interesting that out of the twenty crofts in Marrel, eight were held by women, some of whom were widows.

Too hard a life?

A crofter's wife could find herself left in charge, with the family to bring

Orkney girl at the harvest with the big 'charlie rake'.

up and a croft to run, while her husband was away working all summer and sometimes in winter as well. Fortunately, grandparents were always at hand to keep an eye on children and keeping an older girl off school to help with the little ones was part of the way of life in the west. Many families still needed to be convinced that the kind of education the schools provided was of much use, for girls especially. One Skye farmer, James Scobie of Feorlig, made sure that his local school had a sewing teacher for a start, then he recommended they should have a much wider and more practical training in domestic economy, teaching them to cook and to keep house as well.

'But was the great amount of laborious work women had to do in Skye common also in the Uists, and did it affect their health?' the Commissioners asked Dr Donald Black. He was a middle-aged doctor, trained in Glasgow, and a good Gaelic-speaker who acted as their interpreter at Lochboisdale. Dr Black agreed the Uist women did a lot of hard work loading carts, pulling barrows and carrying seaweed in creels on their backs — but the people kept horses, perhaps too many; and because of this he had not seen much of harrowing with the hand. He had no doubt that the health of some women did suffer due to the labour they performed. Pregnant women in his experience kept on working up to near the time when their baby was born, but after it they generally did little housework for a fortnight or so. When Lord Napier asked him if the labour of the women was imposed on them by idleness on the part of the men or was it entirely in the nature of things, Dr Black replied that it was in the nature of things — the women were obliged to labour. What the women felt about their lives and their share of the work on the croft, the Commissioners had few opportunities to discover. Almost without exception all the witnesses who appeared before them were men.

Other Work, Home and Away

The cry the Commissioners heard everywhere, at least until they reached Sanday in Orkney, was that crofts were too small to keep a family, and if in addition no alternative work was to be had, people could not help running short of food. That is why the requirement placed on some cottars to work on their neighbouring farm whenever the farmer wanted them was in one way welcome, because it did give them an opportunity to earn. On John Scott's farm of Drynoch in Skye, for example, this could mean 1s.6d. a day for doing fieldwork for fifteen to twenty days a year, and 2s. a day for mowing or harrowing or cleaning drains for another twenty or thirty days — not the highest rates of pay but wages in money for working near home. At Barr overlooking Loch Teachuis in Morvern the farmer, Captain J. T. Shaw, also paid 2s. a day, and 2s.6d. when men couldn't get home at night, and provided work for about fifty days in the year. He expected cottars to come at lambing and clipping times, but they were free to work elsewhere at other times if they thought they could earn more money. No better employment was to be had locally and, Malcolm MacLachlan their spokesman said, 'We are very thankful when we get the work.'

Fishing at home
Herring

'We fish about the place', was how one of the Letterfearn crofters put it. Most of them had only one acre of land and some had none. In the last few years some of them had started going together to Loch Hourn in bigger boats, which a local carpenter built for them at Dornie. By fishing for a merchant who gave them goods on credit and bought their fish they avoided any worry over marketing their catch. Three others fishing in Loch Duich had only four barrels to sell, which they themselves sent on the steamer to Glasgow and had no idea how much they would fetch. Donald Fraser, the teacher and inspector of the poor at Glenelg and James Milligan, the farmer of Arnisdale both agreed that it was the Loch Hourn fishing that saved the whole district from starvation.

Many places, Lochinver for example and the west of Skye, needed quays where fishing boats could shelter and unload their catches. The Commissioners had noticed in Skye the boats had to be small because each was hauled up into a little dock (sometimes called a *noust*) which its owner had scooped out for it on the shore. With better piers and harbours, whole crews from Skye who had their own bigger boats could begin to compete against boats from the north-east in western waters. As we have seen already, the herring boom in Barra and Lewis gave island men the opportunity to make up the crews on the north-east boats to full strength and earn wages while fishing at home in early summer, although in Lewis many more of the boats involved were local. In Shetland fishermen had never been so busy or so prosperous and Orkney too was sharing in the new interest in herring. The number of boats in Orkney might be only half what it used to be, 200 or 206 compared with about

400 but now they were far more valuable and bigger boats. The fishing was mainly for herring now, with some white fishing and curing still.

A noust, a shelter for a boat on Skye.

Lobsters

Although in Soay south of Skye, as Alexander MacCaskill testified, they had only a creek where the entrance was dry at low water, all their earnings and much of their food came from fishing. They didn't go to Loch Hourn for herrings, John MacRae another islander said, because they had no nets. He fished for lobsters for about three months in the year and got 5s. a dozen for them when they were plentiful and 7s. when they were scarce. Hector MacKenzie a cottar at Solitote in the north of Skye said he and his neighbour might have a dozen or a dozen and a half lobsters on a good day and taking the winter over, perhaps six or seven. The most he ever made from lobsters in a season was about £10 and the least about £4 or £5. His lobsters went to Portree bound for London. When he finished with them in the spring it was time to turn back to the land, to plant his potatoes and cast his peats, then he would be off to the east coast fishing on 1st July. Up on the north coast, for example at Melness west of Tongue, getting lobsters to market was too difficult. They had to be taken first to Thurso by road or by boat as there was no regular steamer or trading smack, or sixty miles in a cart to the railway station at Lairg.

Salmon

According to Roderick MacInnes of Glasbheinn and Norman Stewart of Valtos there was regular work at the salmon fishing in the summer for about a hundred men in the north-east of Skye. Working four men to every boat they earned 10s.6d. a week and a percentage of the fish caught. The season lasted about four months to the end of August and when the fishing was good they could finish up with £10 to £14. This fish too went to Portree by steamer.

Gathering whelks

Sometimes people had nothing to eat but shell-fish. Alexander MacCaskill said this happened for a fortnight in 1833 in Soay. At other times people in the island gathered them to sell. They had to take them a long way to Loch Slapin by boat, and pay a cart to take them on to Broadford. For a bag containing about four bushels, the produce of two spring tides, they might get 10s. In many other coastal communities gathering them was done by the children and the poor: it was an occupation of the last resort.

Crafts

It is often assumed to be universally true that it was better to be a crofter than a cottar simply because the crofter had some land. Certainly many of the poorest people were cottars, but many others were the people who had those special skills a township or a district depended on for services they needed and could not perform for themselves. Having no land their trade was their means of living and they had all their time to give to it. Their skills brought some variety to the local economy. A blacksmith, for example, had a place in an agricultural community to make and mend tools and cooking utensils, and to shoe horses, which Donald MacIver did at Cross of Ness in Lewis in 1883 for 3s. a set or just 9d. a shoe. So had the shoemaker like John MacCaskill of Fernilea in Skye who charged more for shoes for humans, 12s. for men's shoes and 9s. for women's, and 17s. for men's boots and 12s. for women's. Some crafts such as weaving and tailoring were in decline in the face of machine-made cloth and ready-made clothes from the south, but, as we have seen, a woman was still making pottery for everyday use in Lewis.

How much is to be learned about the range of skills of craftspeople depends on the local knowledge and conscientiousness of the factors who made the Returns about them. For Pennyghael in Mull, for example, the information sometimes covers more than one occupation. Archibald MacNeill who had the Post Office for instance, was also a road surfacer, and Duncan Lamont was a 'shoemaker, piper etc.', suggesting probably that he was paid sometimes for playing his bagpipes. John MacDonald of Newton in North Uist was a particularly good recorder. Knockline, he noted, had two merchants, two tailors, two blacksmiths (father and son, both called Angus MacDonald) a joiner, a shoemaker, a herd and a weaveress, while among people's occupations at Carinish he recorded Angus MacDonald as a carrier and Rachel MacDonald as another weaveress.

In the smithy at Cornaigbeg on Tiree.

There were signs of more specialised skills in the Ross of Mull where Archibald MacDonald of Tirighoil was a cartwright, Robert Graham of Bunessan a wheel-turner and Hugh Cameron of Assapol a boat-builder. Lachlan Black of Kentra, who was a mason was also described as a stone dresser and in Tirighoil two men had work connected with animals, Malcolm MacFarlane as a shepherd and Angus MacMaster as a cattle drover, who would take cattle landing from islands such as Tiree along the drove road to Grass Point for the crossing to Oban.

Transport

Glenelg on the coast of Inverness-shire also had a boat-builder, John MacLean, as well as a sail-maker, Ewen MacLure, while in Knoydart Betsey Robertson was described as 'a saillery woman'. Not surprisingly in Glenelg, where cattle came over on the important ferry route from Skye

A boat full of cattle at Kyleakin, Skye early this century.

Sheep being transported on the Gondolier along the Caledonian Canal.

(and Lewis and the Uists) both Donald MacLeod and Ewen MacPherson were cattle drovers and Alexander MacLeod a ferryman. Over on the other side at Kylerhea, Donald Martin, was one of five who had to be constantly on hand to man the boat and ferry the cattle across. The toll for each animal was 6d., the crew got half of that between them and the inn-keeper got the other half. There was a time, he said, when they would make £13 or £14 in the year but now they would make no more than £5 a year because so many of the animals were being carried by steamer and train. One sign of how far droving had declined was that he and the other crofters now grazed a cow on the stance where the droves used to rest. At Lochbroom William Cameron, parish minister there for forty years, complained of a man who kept far too many sheep on the land he let to him and never paid any rent at all. What irritated the minister particularly was that the man could afford to pay — 'He had been doing a good deal in the way of droving and it is not with an empty hand a man can drove in this country.'

Wheelwrights like Alexander MacDonell in North Morar played a part in supplying vehicles for the road, while others found work as contractors or surfacemen in maintaining the roads. Up at Rogart in Sutherland where previously men had flocked to work constructing the railway, 'railway surfaceman' appeared as a new occupation involved in maintaining it. Among the cottars who found work on the Caledonian Canal Robert Cassels was a canal porter at Corpach and Alexander MacNaughton a lock-keeper at Banavie.

Construction and extraction

There was not much work for masons in building houses, because of the tradition that crofters built their own but when public works were being carried out, like the harbour at Lybster at the time the Commissioners met there in 1883, masons and a good many labourers were employed. Interestingly, the Commissioners interviewed a mason at Lybster, called Alexander Sutherland from Roster of Clyth, who used to be away working in Edinburgh but had found plenty of work back in Caithness for the last ten years.

'There have been any amount of schools to build (for school boards after the Education Act of 1872). Our wages have increased and diminished again with the schools being finished. There was seldom such a thing happening as so many buildings going on.'

Building programmes everywhere created a demand for stone, and

Ruins of the old lime-kilns and workmen's houses by the jetty at An Sailean, Lismore.

quarries, where the work was regular but hard, tended to be close to the sea. At Castletown close to the north coast, men quarrying Caithness flags for export earned 2s. to 2s.4d. for a ten hour day. Workers in the quarries in Mull were paid rather more, 15s. to £1 for a full week, according to John MacCormick of Catchean, much the same as in the lime quarries in Lismore but the number of workers was small and they had to be strong, able-bodied men.

Work was also to be had cutting peats to be exported from Eday in Orkney. Being very good peats they were in demand from distilleries in the south and a schooner always came to collect them. Adam Hoon, the factor, described the arrangements:

'They cut them, prepare them and ship them on board ships. We pay them 19s. a fathom: ten years ago it was 15s. There is no other work for a man to do then, at a season of the year when his croft is laid down. The women and children help in spreading and drying the peats; the men cut them and drive them down in carts. We sell about 1000 tons to the distillers. That comes to about 12s. a ton and leaves 6s. after paying freight on the schooner.'

In the Uists the boom time which had brought high incomes to those who made kelp was long past. Nobody wanted it any more, but over in Tiree there was a demand for sea-tangle which crofters could collect for E. C. Stamford's iodine-making factory. As his main plant was not in the island, however but on the Clyde, the number of people he employed directly was very small and this was typical of the Highlands generally, where there were very few manufacturing industries where people could find work.

No.	NAME.	On a Croft.	Not on a Croft.	Amount. £	s.	d.	To whom paid, Proprietor or Tenant.	Occupation or Means of Subsistence.
							Payable to	
1	Angus McDonald Jr.		Actonfooft.		10		Proprietor	Carrier
2	Robert Ferguson		"		10		"	Labourer
3	Mary McKinnon		'		5		"	Wood.
4	Arch McDonald Hs	On Croft.		1			"	Joiner
5	Neil McPherson		Actonfooft.		5		"	Carpenter
6	Mary McRury.		"		5		"	Milk gatherer
7	Isabella McDonald		"		2	6		"
8	Lachlan McLean		"	2			"	Shoemaker
9	Widow Rachel McDonald.		"		r			Weaveress.
10	Alexr McDonald		'		-	-		Agricultural labour

ROYAL COMMISSION (HIGHLANDS AND ISLANDS.)
RETURN RESPECTING COTTARS — Carinish — No. 1

Estate of *North Uist* the Property of *Sir J.W.P Campbell-Orde Bart* at the 1st day of January 1883.

Signed *McDonald*
Address *Newton Lochmady*
Date *3r May 1883*

The range of work among cottars at Carinish, North Uist in 1883.

Postal services and tourism

The extension of the postal services provided some employment all over the Highlands and Islands. In Shetland, for example, Thomas Henderson of Olnafirth, Delting, who had both the grandfathers living in his house along with his wife and child, was thankful to have been 'running postman for the last five years' to augment his little croft. Far away at Galltair near Glenelg the post route the messenger had to negotiate from Lochalsh was only a sheep track, very treacherous in wet weather when he might have 30lbs. on his back. The Commissioners heard this in the first week of the new parcel post service in Britain but so far nobody in Little Galltair had received a parcel and nobody had sent one! Others had post offices. Sometimes the person in charge was a woman, like Jessie MacDonald who was postmistress and telegraph operator at Sandside in the far north of Caithness.

So far the impact of summer visitors on crofting communities was not great because tourists tended to travel on well-defined routes to well known places. To illustrate this, a crofter on Iona might see a future for good cottages to let on his island (page 83) whereas when a shopkeeper at Carbost in the west of Skye was asked about his earnings from tourists, he replied simply, 'Very few tourists come this length.'

Nonetheless, the variety of occupations in the Highlands was astonishing. The Returns show that at Port Skerra on the north coast one man was a boots in a hotel in summer, one in Arisaig was a footman, one in Latheron in Caithness a book canvasser — none of them occupations which spring to mind immediately associated with the designation 'cottar'.

Public appointments

Any additional employment would be taken up by somebody, if it could be carried out from home. When Duncan MacKay of Duirinish in Lochalsh was asked if he lived entirely from the produce of his land he replied proudly, 'Oh no, I'm sheriff officer.' Unfortunately because the total number of alternative jobs available was so very small, considerable resentment was aroused when all the public appointments were monopolised by one family. This happened in Durness where the ground officer was the only meal dealer in the parish. His daughter was the female teacher, his son-in-law was the teacher and registrar, his son and younger daughter were pupil teachers and he himself was the compulsory officer ('the school board man'). The factor agreed that all this was true but he put it down to no more than the daughter 'happening to marry' the local teacher.

Professor MacKinnon summed up the lack of opportunity in the Highlands very well by taking the image of the ladder of life. 'The Highland ladder', he said, 'has only two rungs — one at the bottom where the great mass of people are, and one at the top where there were only very few, and it is almost impossible to leap from one to the other.' Crofting families had no chance of improving themselves by moving from a small croft to a large croft and on to a small or medium-sized farm on the one hand, or by remunerative public employment close to their homes on the other.

Work away from home

Going away to work for several months of the year was part of the pattern of life in Skye, so much so that Neil MacPherson of Gedentailor in the Braes regarded his croft as simply a home to come back to from the fishing at Kinsale or the east coast. It was by fishing that they earned enough to pay the rent and feed their families. Usually they were away

For want of a habour the St Kilda men unloading stores from a ship on to the rocks, 1896.

eight to ten weeks, but his usual practice was to be away at work most of the year. Hector MacKenzie of Solitote supplied details of his earnings from fishing. As a hired man he got £7 for the season, and 1s. per cran in addition. The fewest he had had was 130 crans and the highest 272 crans. James Grant, the minister of Kilmuir, emphaises how many young men and girls too (page 116) went away, and how important it was for their families that they did:

'When the east coast fishing is fairly successful, families who can send sons there may be able to meet their obligations (debts). There is not an unemployed young man left at home during the summer, and many of them go away in winter.'

As far as Skye was concerned crofting as a way of life survived only because of money earned elsewhere.

Some crofters elsewhere could fish for a longer season. John Fraser, a crofter from Gartymore near Helmsdale, who had been going away since he was sixteen, hired himself usually at places like Peterhead and Fraserburgh and fished off the Aberdeen coast for about ten weeks. Then he had another seven weeks at the herring fishing near home.

Neighbours of his went to other work, he said, 'for whiles in the year'. They had worked on constructing the railway to the north until 1874, some went south, and a few had been employed at the gold diggings (in Kildonan). His own brother, a mason, had gone to America to work for the season. This was not unusual in the north. Donald MacKenzie, Free Church minister of Farr for the last thirteen years, drew attention to eight to a dozen young men, heads of families, who were in the habit of doing this:

'They crossed the Atlantic and worked there for a season and then came home. One of them who had learned his trade in building said he had never earned on the Duke's estate more than 3s.6d., and that was for putting a grate in a public school! There is no work here.'

A good number went south to agricultural work. Over in Gairloch, Dr Charles Robertson, who had been there since the potato famine, reckoned 'About fifty go south to work for every one that went at that time. They go to all parts of the country — to Ross, Moray, Banff, and even Ayrshire, and some to Roxburghshire. Young women go too. Most go in May to the feeing markets and stay for six months. They contribute considerably to the support of their families.'

A doctor in Skye believed there were no better navvies than Skyemen and hinted that this might be in part be due to their food when they were away working, because he added, 'But then they're having their beef three times a day.' They took to railway work, several having been employed on the Callander and Oban Railway, and they were also good roadmen. The Commissioners met an exceptional one at Uig: he was Donald Beaton of Earlish who was still going away to work at the age of 74. From spring to summer every year he would be working on the roads in Kintyre, where he got 2s.6d. a day and his lodging, wages which could not be equalled in Skye.

In Islay where Free Church minister John G. MacNeil who was a native of the island claimed the villagers of Portnahaven were the poorest he knew in all the Islands, the custom was to go away to work in the wintertime. 'Were it not for the proximity of the Glasgow shipyards where they get work in winter,' he said, 'they would perish with hunger.'

Because it was only for the season that most Highlanders went away to work, only relatively unskilled work was open to them. And in it they were always the labourers, never the supervisors. If they wanted to follow a career, they had to stay away and work full-time, like the numbers of Orcadians who went to the 'Hudson's Bay Company', or islanders like James Beaton, retired master mariner of Tobermory, whose career had taken him on long sea voyages on sailing ships all over the world. Nearer home Glasgow was a place where tens of thousands of Highlanders went to settle because they could find work, particularly in the shipyards, and a good many became policemen in the Glasgow force.

Domestic Life

The House
Building the house

The walls of the house wrapped round the lives of the family, its roof gave them shelter, and usually it was the crofter himself who built it. He built the walls of stone and sometimes he credited the stones themselves with human qualities. Donald Martin of Tolsta did when he recalled, 'Last spring I began to waken up stones to erect a new house.' On their first day in Skye John Mathieson of Achnahannet told the Commissioners a great deal about how he had built his house (a *black house*). He needed six *couples* (pairs of matching timbers) to give the house its shape and hold up the roof. These might be about 4 inches (10cm.) in diameter and were set 6 feet apart. He bought them over in Raasay and they cost him £1. It took six or seven weeks to build his house, with help from his neighbours at times but never for a full day because he didn't pay them. His other expenditure was 6s. for a door, 3s. for a second-hand window with four panes and, unusually, 1s.6d. for a little roof window as well.

Getting materials other than stones was difficult in out-of-the-way places, as Donald MacDonald, an old Mull crofter recollected. He had had to send a man to Lismore to get lime before he could start: then he built a barn and a byre as well as a house. When he was removed from his croft twenty years later, materials he had supplied himself had become part of the structure and what irritated him most was having 'to leave my sash windows, twelve panes in each, and not get a single sixpence for them, and I had to buy two common windows', which presumably would not open.

Building houses with stone and lime (*white houses*) was becoming more common and Shetlanders appreciated that they saved them being 'blown from the fireside', on windy nights. At Acharacle in Ardnamurchan Charles Cameron explained that his house was built all through with lime and not just pointed with it, yet he had neighbours who were still living in houses built solely of turf, no better than the houses the first settlers built at Locheport in North Uist.

In Caithness where the stone was excellent for building, Alexander Sutherland the mason said the old croft houses were all built with stone and clay and might be pointed with lime only on the outside. A house like that, he said, would last a hundred years and would not fall down. Elsewhere houses did need a lot of attention. When Roderick MacInnes of Glasbheinn in the north of Skye was asked how much he had put into improving his house, he replied simply, 'It fell once and I rebuilt it.'

Inside a black house, the floor was usually of clay and very often the fire was in the middle. The *Scotsman* correspondent was as critical of houses in Barra as the *Daily Mail*'s man was of houses in Glendale because so many had no chimneys or even holes in the roof, and the smoke belched out the door. One proprietor in Skye, Lachlan MacDonald of Skeabost who tried to encourage people to use chimney cans, accepted that they could give good reasons for preferring to keep the fire in the centre, 'Because they can sit round it and warm themselves when they have not a change of clothing.' Captain Allan MacDonald of Waternish, another Skye proprietor, tried to persuade his people to build a middle wall in each house with a chimney in it but when he went into houses to have a look, he found the fire still in the centre of the floor, 'where they say they can get round it.' This was the usual position in Harris too where a young factor expressed the locally-held view that the smoke kept the people warm, and his own that thatched houses were warmer than most slated houses. In the island of Foula too, most of the fires were in the middle of the floor.

Boxbeds, central hearth, paraffin lamp on left in an Orkney house early this century.

A few crofters would employ a mason to build them a house but Donald Martin a mason in Lewis found crofters had become too poor to afford his very modest charges. He would build the gable and the walls, 12 feet long, of the dwelling part of the house for £2 or the whole 60 feet length of the building to include the barn and the byre for £10. Lachlan MacDonald was one landowner in Skye who had better houses with two rooms and a closet built for only £10 to £15. It was common for a proprietor to give the timbers for the roof, which was essential in a place like Foula. In Easter Ross the proprietor gave the wood only for the couples, according to Angus Forbes of Highfield Park, who complained that he himself had to pay for the sawing and the carting from the forest to the sawmill. Sometimes nature provided: as Donald Martin of Tolsta, Lewis explained, 'Driftwood comes ashore here sometimes which is roofing.'

Where the landowners took the initiative in building, this usually produced better houses. D. C. Edmonston in Shetland claimed a two-roomed house of stone and lime could be built for as little as £20 provided the tenant agreed to put the turf and thatch on top, while in Orkney Benjamin Swanson reckoned most of the houses in North Ronaldsay had two rooms, chimneys and wooden partitions, and some had wooden floors. But costs could rise beyond the means of both the landlord and the tenant. John Bruce, younger of Sumburgh in Shetland quoted a price of £120 to build a decent three-roomed slated cottage which would require the tenant to pay £6 a year extra in rent, because he said, 'A landlord cannot afford to be a philanthropist in stone and lime.'

The practice of whitening the outside of houses seems to have originated with landlords who supplied the material. 'The landlord gives us lime to put on the outside,' said Thomas Henderson of Whalsay in Shetland and then he complained, 'but we must put it on.' And in Iona, as we have seen (page 82), Malcolm Ferguson was not sure whether their houses were black or white houses — they were whitewashed anyhow, he said, with the Duke of Argyll's whitewash!

Roofing the house

Keeping the inside dry in a wet climate was a constant worry to the people living in the house. To John Ross a young crofter of Gruids near Lairg, there was no easy answer.

'If it rains outside for three hours, it rains inside for six! These are thatched houses. There is no slate. We cannot renew the thatch unless we use our straw and that means less food for our own cattle. The original thatch was turf; that might last a year or so, but whenever the turf is done it is as bad as ever.'

Mending the roof at Poolewe; note the heap of material and who carried it.

Divot roofs were still common on old houses in Caithness, Sutherland and Shetland. David MacKenzie, minister of Farr at the time of the Sutherland clearances, recorded in 1818 that his barn, byre, stable and kiln had been recently roofed with divots in this customary way but were again in ruins. He argued against this kind of roofing, saying that because it didn't last, the damp seeped through and weakened the walls and that cutting new turf to replace it was a waste of scarce pasture. David Petrie, whose house at Gossaburgh in Mid Yell had a divot roof, reckoned it was 'not fit for a human being to live under.'

But thatch was the most common material used on roofs. It needed to be patched or replaced frequently, usually when the house was empty with the women and children up at the shieling. The materials, straw as a rule, or rushes, were not easy to obtain and Angus Stewart of Peinchorran and Donald MacKinnon of Elgol in Skye both admitted to the Commission that they had had to steal rushes in the past. Heather thatch didn't last long either, and heather ropes were often made to stop the thatch from blowing away. 'Anyone who knows about these houses, thatched with heather,' insisted General Burroughs of Rousay, 'knows it is necessary to put a new roof on every year.' Although heather might appear to be so plentiful as to have no financial value in the Highlands and Islands, crofters were not at liberty to pull it at any time they liked. Murdo MacLean of Valtos in Lewis claimed that the gamekeepers set apart one day only in the year when crofters might freely pull the heather. Later he corrected this to 'three days in one particular week in the year', but the restrictions stood at other times when anyone pulling heather might be reported and fined.

In 1883, felt roofs were becoming all the rage in Shetland. A wooden roof covered with felt, according to John Omand of Mid Yell, 'would answer as well as slate and be lighter,' and older men, Matthew Robertson and James Barclay the minister living in the same place, agreed that it was much superior to thatch for keeping out the rain. When it came to maintaining it, Matthew much preferred the prospect of tarring it regularly to rethatching and he expected his felt roof to last a lifetime.

With a felt roof still in 1975 on the house at Hamnavoe, Northmavine of Johnny Williamson, a pioneer of vaccination.

Slates generally appeared on new houses which a landowner employed a mason to build, although some crofters managed to replace their thatch with slate. Peter MacKay, an 80-year-old crofter at Strathtongue who had been a builder and a slater in his day, revealed their secret: they had dutiful sons. 'A few people', he maintained, 'who were getting better up in the world by having dutiful sons, got their houses slated'.

Cattle and people under the same roof

Crofters' houses were commonly criticised because the people and their cattle were often under the same roof and came in by the same door. John MacKenzie admitted that it was like this at Annat of Torridon, where he lived: the houses were 'old reekies of two or three apartments, the third occupied by the cow and the hens entering by the same door as the human inmates.' In old houses on the Forse estate west of Lybster in Caithness, George Sinclair explained that an old sail was put up to separate the animals from the fire but Charles MacKenzie MacRae, a doctor in Stornoway had no strong disapproval of cattle and people living under the same roof since these were long houses and the cattle lived at one end (and usually down the slope), provided the drainage outside was kept in good order. His objection was that people often 'have the part where the cattle are, excavated to retain the manure and it retains the oozing and liquid that should be removed.'

As a landlord Sir John Campbell Orde tried to prevent new houses being built in North Uist where people and cattle would be living under the same roof, while at Barvas in Lewis where the landlord insisted on a division being erected between the house and the byre, and actually supplied two outside doors, one for the house and one for the byre, the chamberlain William MacKay discovered that in no time at all the doors had been closed up (probably to reduce draughts) and that a single door again served to admit both people and cattle.

Room inside

With large numbers in so many families, houses which had only one or two rooms as a rule, must have been very crowded. One-roomed houses measuring 14 feet to 12 feet each way at Bonavoulin near Lochaline, for example, could be divided up by the way the beds were arranged and also had a loft where a bed could be placed, but in the village of Lochaline itself where most of the houses also had just one room with no partition and no loft, some of the villagers actually took in lodgers. Most was heard about the closed wooden beds called *boxbeds* in Orkney where Archibald MacCallum the young Free Church minister of Rousay referred to them making a partition between one end of the house and the other, and W. T. Dennison regarded them as 'perhaps the greatest improvement in the domestic economy at the end of the eighteenth century.' He remembered sheltering in a storm in 1847 in a little house, 14 feet by 12, where a cottar and his wife and six children lived. Seeing only one bed in the house he asked where they all slept.

'Weel, the wife and I lie wi' our heeds at the head o' the bed, the twa eldest lie wi' their heeds at the foot o' the bed, the peerie t'ing — that's the baby — lies i' his mither's bosom, the ain next the peerie t'ing lies i' mine, and the middle twa lie on a shelf in the foot o' the bed, over the heads o' the eldest twa. An' trath I can tell you we are no cauld gin (if) I close the bed doors. But gin the eldest ain is no growin' sae lang, that miny a time he gaes me a box wi' his foot under the chin'.

Measuring this boxbed, Dennison found it was only 5 feet 8 inches long, 3 feet 10 inches wide and 4 feet 8 inches from the bedboards to its roof! By 1883, however, he reckoned crofters had houses with two, and sometimes three rooms, 'one fitted up as the best room with a wooden floor, a grate in the fireplace, curtains, blinds and geraniums in the window.' But the greatest advance since then in his opinion came from having new oil lamps and cheap paraffin to burn in them, which extended their days and enriched their lives by lighting up the house on the long winter evenings.

Food and drink

Because of the purpose of their inquiry the Royal Commission, having learned more about houses than housework, also learned more about items of food than the cooking of them. Frequently crofters reminded them of how basic and burdensome the getting of food was. At Sangobeg on the north coast, for example, where no one had a horse, Alexander Morrison explained:

'A man must go first to the seaware and then to the spade; he must sow the seed and then harrow the ground after that, and go three-quarters of a mile up the hill for a creel of peat to make a fire that will make ready his breakfast.'

In most places the amount of grain-growing was declining and as a result many corn mills were reported to be falling out of use in Skye and the Outer Isles, but querns (hand mills) were said to be still in use in houses in Lewis. A boll of oats and a boll of barley was all John MacIver of Breasclete, could send to the mill in a year: he had to buy in meal for his animals and the family. Potatoes, his main crop, would see them through the winter in a good year but last year the crop was hardly worth lifting.

'In the mornings now', he said, 'the Breasclete people have porridge, out of meal from Stornoway, and some more or less of bread just as it comes. Everyone that can takes tea.

'For dinner the one that can have tea will have it. There is no milk. With it they take bread and those who fish may have more or less of fish.'

The amount of tea-drinking aroused controversy. Generally the crofters accepted that they all drank too much of it and some of their critics could become quite vehement on the subject, none more than Roderick MacLean, factor to Sir Alexander Matheson of Lochalsh. He claimed in public that slushes of tea were destroying their nervous systems and threatening the survival of the race of the Gael! Then in a letter he asserted that 'insanity among the poorer classes is on the increase and I attribute much of it to the excess of tea-drinking without enough food.' The evidence of doctors restored a sense of balance. Dr Charles Robertson, who was the doctor in Gairloch for twenty-five years, did not think tea was being drunk to such an extent as to be harmful, and Dr Alexander Buchanan, who had been almost as long in Tiree, attributed people's new habits with food — drinking tea and coffee twice a day and

The Barvas potter's response to the fashion for drinking tea.

consuming more baker's bread and wheaten flour — to changes in fashion and good communications with the towns in the south. 'Gentlemen now have taken to porridge and milk,' he observed, 'and the poorer classes have taken to tea and coffee.'

Doctors did worry that children did not get nearly enough milk, because calves which crofters needed to rear and sell in order to pay the rent, had first claim on their mother's milk. Winter and spring were the worst times when cows were kept indoors. If they were let out, it was not to graze, Alexander Walker, an Aberdeen fish merchant discovered in Shetland, as there was scarcely any grass but 'to get the air'; and later through lack of food, they could not get up by themselves and needed to be lifted. He referred to syrup being bought as a substitute for milk for children in Shetland, like the treacle John MacPherson mentioned in Glendale. Dr A. D. Fraser in Skye worried because he was convinced of the link between disease and lack of food, and the solution Dr Black advocated in South Uist, giving cheap beer which would be nourishing instead of tea to two- or three-year-old children, caused some consternation when it was reported in the press.

Potatoes, salted herrings and imported meal were the food of the people in winter. The commonest complaint according to Dr Fraser was dyspepsia, caused by eating too much meal and hardly any other kind of food. He told people they needed variety in their diet, fish which was nutritious and their own eggs which they should not sell for tea, but avoiding eating eggs was a custom on islands from Skye to Foula where they could be sold to reduce one's debts or be exchanged for goods in the local shop.

Not much detail emerged on food prices. Tea at 3s. per pound at Fernilea in Skye was slightly dearer than the tea sold in Foula, and meal at Fernilea sold for 24s. a boll or 3s. a stone of 17½ lbs., much the same as the fish-curers were charging in Lewis. Loch Fyne fishermen were pioneers in using foods which would keep on their boats such as tinned beef and tinned milk. From James MacLardy in Tarbert they were in the habit of ordering 'tea, sugar, perhaps a little coffee, preserved milk, preserved beef and wheaten bread.'

Old Donald in Colonsay cutting his potatoes ready for planting.

By the fireside on Bressay, Shetland, 1889.

Whisky

In several places mention was made of *sma' stills* where people made their own whisky. The factor of the Forse estate in Caithness defended evictions he carried out at Stemster where he found a false wall inside a house concealing the place where the distilling had taken place. Mull also saw evictions for making whisky, while others suffered for selling whisky in *shebeens,* for example in Kintail. In Skye people used to make their own, later they bought home-made whisky from the Gairloch people who were still producing it in 1884 according to the newspapers. Obviously a satisfied customer, John MacLean of Hallin Park called them 'very kind people, the Gairloch people'. When a distillery at Carbost began to produce Talisker, a malt whisky which became famous, local people didn't drink it. 'Not a gill of it is drunk here,' a Carbost merchant explained. 'it's too dear. We get our whisky from Greenock or Glasgow.'

Hints that sma' stills were a part of life and the local economy in quite recent times were given by an incomer to Tiree and a Lewisman. Edward Charles Stanford arrived in Tiree to consider setting up a factory in 1863 but since he was a stranger, they believed he was an excise officer. Thinking he was on the look-out for illicit stills they shunned him and would do nothing for him, a sign surely that they knew that home-made whisky was still being distilled on the island. There was certainly a demand for it, since Hugh MacDiarmid, the sub-factor admitted 'there was no public house on the island, not one licence in the place'.

In Lewis John Nicolson who was 69, remembered four sma' stills working in Shawbost and smuggling going on:

'In addition to maintaining our families by the produce of our crofts,' he said, 'we were able to send to those small stills more or less of barley every year, when they used to make whisky and sell it for 2s.6d. a pint of three bottles. I mention the distilling just to show Shawbost was productive at that time!'

The churches were against strong drink, the Free Church especially, and the Temperance movement, in whose hall at Tobermory the Royal Commission held one of its meetings, was very active in the Highlands. Alexander Davidson, Free Church minister of South Harris for thirty years, was one who claimed they had shut out alcohol from his parish altogether:

'There are no shebeens as far as I know, and we are most thankful that there is no public house. Strong drink is not sold in any part at this end.' When Sheriff Nicolson said he thought there was a public house at Obbe, Mr Davidson replied,

'Not now, it is discontinued and we are very thankful for it.'

Other ministers appeared to be more tolerant. Some, like James R. Sutherland of Northmavine in Shetland for example who claimed that in thirty-five years in the parish he had never seen a drunken man, were more concerned about the effects of tea. And on St Kilda where the minister John MacKay appeared to have strict control over nearly everything in people's lives, he accepted that people would have a bottle or two of whisky in the house and would like to take a glass after coming home from the hill. 'Young men,' said Roderick MacLeod for nearly thirty years minister of South Uist, 'may occasionally take a "spree" at weddings, markets and formerly (but not now) at funerals; and like all men of Celtic idiosyncrasies get very much excited and make a great noise, but as a class Highland crofters, to my certain knowledge, are a sober lot.'

Entertainments

'There is no music now among the people, not one piper in all Duirinish.'
The Commission heard this in Skye from Alexander MacKenzie who
lived at Boreraig, the township which had been the seat of the famous
piping family, the MacCrimmons, as the hereditary pipers to the
MacLeods. When he was asked why, he replied, 'I believe it is the Gospel
that has done away with the pipe; it was death that did away with the
MacCrimmons'.

John Munro who ran a non-sectarian mission on South Rona,
remembered *ceilidhs* when people met and told stories and sang songs but
these had been given up and now he did not know a single piper on
Raasay. He agreed that their going was due to the influence of Free
Church ministers but he also felt 'it was leading to folly'.

Captain Allan MacDonald of Waternish was one who missed the
singing: 'I must say I like to hear them sing a song. When they used to
manufacture kelp, it was pretty in the evening to hear them crossing in
their boats and singing songs as they rowed along. And they used to sing
songs when reaping the harvest too, but not now; I think the clergy rather
discourage it. Some songs, though, were abused — young men when they
sang songs of that kind, might be found carrying a bottle of whisky in
their pocket.'

Remembering balls and dances at times like Christmas in his young
days when they used to have bagpipe music and plenty of songs from
both men and women, old John MacLean of Hallin Park agreed that
people had fewer *ceilidhs* now but besides blaming ministers, who 'won't
be for the like of that at all,' he put much of it down to poverty. 'When a
man is depressed with poverty,' he believed, 'he cannot be cheerful.'

Moment of beauty, a view in North Uist.

Transport and travel

Some people had difficulties in transporting things, others in travelling from one place to another. None of the crofters in Annat of Torridon for instance had a horse or cart or a plough: the boat and the creel took their place:

'The boat is the sea-cart, carrying the sea-ware to the shore; the creel is the next cart, carrying from the shore to the field.'

This meant that people accepted that they had to walk long distances on land and carry things on their backs. The people of Scarp, for example, who bought all their provisions in Tarbert would have welcomed a road with an even surface to walk on, and in many places the same complaint was constantly being made — 'We pay road money but we have no road.'

In Sangobeg near Durness isolation was highlighted because the crofters had no horses, as Alexander Morrison explained:

At present we are 31 miles from a doctor who lives in Scourie. We have to send a foot messenger for him and it often happens that he cannot be got.'

The doctor served two large parishes and by the time he came a patient could die.

Some Orcadians without horses used oxen instead. George Leonard in Rousay intended to plough with his ox and his neighbour's, and also to put his ox in a cart and harness it, just like a horse. He said the old people did it differently:

'They had a yoke on the ox's neck — a piece of iron round its neck and fastened to the shafts of the cart. I can't say if that was the better way, but I've seen it that way and worked it too.'

He could cart his peats in his ox-cart, which had become the normal way of carrying home the peats in Rousay. Worse off were the Papa Stour people who had to spend three weeks cutting their peats on another island, Papa Little nine miles away, and row them home often over a stormy sea. All over the Highlands and Islands, however, the creel was still handy but only if there was no other way.

Schools and Young Minds

By 1883 the Education Act which aimed to provide schooling for every child had been operating for eleven years. The new buildings it required were there for all to see and the Royal Commission held several of their meetings in them. Nearly every child, even in the remote parts of the Highlands, was now within reach of a school. In Sutherland for example, David Williamson the old minister of Assynt said, 'Education has now reached all, except a few families of gamekeepers and shepherds, and families of that sort.' Although Kildonan a parish covering 210 square miles had only one main school, there were several *side schools* (extra schools in very large parishes) up the Strath to save the children having to walk too far; and in the north round the shores of Loch Eriboll where over a hundred people were living on extremely small crofts, a pupil teacher from Durness School taught in a side school, spending three months on one side of the Loch, then three months on the other.

Going to school

Although nearly all children were on some school roll and more were attending school than ever before, complaints were heard from Skye to Shetland that they didn't attend enough of the time. Duncan Stewart, one of the first schoolmasters the Commissioners encountered in his own school at Stein in Waternish, told them that with a roll of 70 pupils he ought to have an average attendance of 60 but his average was only 43.

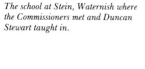
The school at Stein, Waternish where the Commissioners met and Duncan Stewart taught in.

He blamed this on the parents and changes of teachers before him. Illness, snow, the lack of roads and bridges were good reasons for not expecting young children to get to school, and a Shetlander, Thomas Abernethy in Unst, thought children were too young to go to school until they were seven or eight. In winter many children walked to school barefoot, even children who *had* boots came barefoot, Duncan Stewart maintained, but he felt as a teacher he ought not to interfere.

Going home from school in Shetland with umbrellas, shawls and, usually bare feet, 1890.

He didn't know whether they brought anything to eat either:

'I cannot say, for I do not see them eating. I suppose they bring a piece, because they don't go home for dinner. They must have their dinner in their pockets — oatcake and a bit of cheese when they can get it, but no milk. They don't bring any flask or bottle that I have seen. They drink water.'

Work at home was another reason for children staying away from school. It happened now and then on St Kilda when parents wanted the children to go after some cattle, and it happened more regularly in Skye where they stayed off to help with the sowing and planting potatoes in spring and then were needed for various jobs on the croft when their fathers went away to work for the season. Provided the numbers Duncan Stewart gave of the pupils in his older classes, the 5th and 6th Standards — 5 boys and no girls — are not due to some imbalance in the age-group, they may indicate that the parents considered that schooling was more valuable for boys than for girls, or else that girls were more useful at home, minding the house or looking after younger brothers and sisters.

Learning English, not Gaelic

The chief aim in the new schools in Scotland was to teach children to read and write the English language but in the Highlands and Western Isles the mother tongue of the children was Gaelic. Six out of every ten people in Argyll in 1881 were still native speakers of Gaelic, seven out of every ten were in Ross-shire and Inverness-shire, and between seven and eight out of ten in Sutherland, and there were pockets of Gaelic-speakers elsewhere. There was one at Swiney near Lybster in Caithness, for example, which people evicted from Sutherland founded between 1810 and 1820 and where a good sprinkling of Gaelic still survived, according to a 44-year-old witness, himself a Gaelic-speaker. Since Gaelic was the language these children usually heard at home from parents who often could not read or write themselves either in Gaelic or in English, it is not surprising that they would get little help with their lessons at home. They were the first generation of children who nearly all learned to read and write, however, and often crofters like Donald Matheson of Kirkton, Balmacara, for example, told the Royal Commission that the writing down of his township's grievances had been done by a schoolboy.

Not only was English the language taught to young Gaelic-speakers, it was taught *in* English. The case of Duncan Stewart illustrates this well. After teaching in Stirlingshire where he was born, he had come to Stein in Skye where he did not use Gaelic in teaching simply because he could not speak it. His young charges had to try to understand him speaking what was to them a foreign language, whereas he did not understand their Gaelic and they did not dare speak it to him. But teaching them in English created no problems he claimed, 'I find no difficulty in making them understand what I say.' Fortunately many other teachers could speak Gaelic and those who used their Gaelic in teaching English were more successful.

The feeling of the time was in favour of learning English. James Grant of Kilmuir, who had been in the west since 1870 thought parents wanted their children 'to be able to speak English and carve their way through the world' and Andrew Ross, a teacher in Paisley who had been brought up on a croft in Brora, agreed that it was important for all who wanted to leave the Highlands. Recalling the difficulties he had with English as a boy who had been used to speaking only Gaelic, he said he had to think first in Gaelic and then translate into English. He thought it best for children to become used to English from their earliest days.

The teaching of Gaelic did not have many supporters and they were modest in their aims. James Grant of Kilmuir said people wanted it as well as English so that their children would be able to read the Bible in Gaelic. Donald Martin of Tolsta gave the same reason for keeping Gaelic, thinking it could be learned at school along with the English. To the North Uist school board, however, of which John MacDonald of Newton was a member, teaching as much English as possible was the chief aim. When asked if they thought teaching children Gaelic would actually stand in the way of teaching English, he conceded only that if the teacher had plenty of time it would do children no harm to learn their native language.

Once an Inspector of Schools himself, Angus MacPhail a Lewisman writing from Edinburgh, threw off such inhibitions in the way he recommended that education should begin in the child's native language:

'Educate!', he insisted, 'Teach the mother tongue! There is no child in India reading an English book who cannot read his mother tongue, while a man who cannot speak a word of Gaelic may be a schoolmaster in Lewis. The Inspectors may examine in Gaelic if they choose, but these gentlemen not knowing much Gaelic, keep a few phrases as a linguistic curiosity and make them go a long way . . . '

Religious education

Probably Sunday Schools, which were flourishing in many places and teaching the Bible in Gaelic, weakened the case for teaching Gaelic in the board schools as well. In Berneray, for example, 97 children were attending the Sunday School and most of them could read the Bible in Gaelic, according to Malcolm MacLeod, the cottar who (page 75) had written the statement on the condition of the island in Gaelic, not English.

Learning the Bible in Gaelic in the Sunday School and in English in the day school from someone else left the difficulties of translating and reconciling any differences with those least able to cope with them, the children themselves. In Lewis John MacDonald a crofter of South Dell reckoned that religious education in the board school was just a name and that the children did not understand what they were learning:

Lord Napier: 'Do they learn the Shorter Catechism?'
John MacDonald: 'A little bit at the beginning — the easy bit.'
Lord Napier: 'Do they learn it in English or Gaelic?'
John MacDonald: 'Oh! what but in English which they don't understand'.
Lord Napier: 'Do they learn to read the Bible in Gaelic?'
John MacDonald: 'No, not at all.'

The young teacher at Lionel, John Munro, who admitted that he couldn't speak Gaelic fluently, agreed that all the religious instruction was in English and that the Shorter Catechism was in most cases learned by rote, only the more intelligent of the children being able to understand it. Children who had no English at all, he said, started to learn the Shorter Catechism and to read the simplest parts of the Bible.

The costs of education

Although it was compulsory, education was not yet free. In Duncan Stewart's school in Skye, the lowest fee was 1s. a quarter 'for all the youngest child can take in,' rising to 1s.3d. in Standard 1 and by 3d. a year to 2s. a quarter in Standards 1V and above for 'the three R's; and for 7s.6d. a quarter a few pupils who stayed on could take extra subjects, Latin, French, Geometry, Algebra and Drawing. All the fees went to the teacher.

Some people, like Evander MacIver, the Sutherland factor for example, criticised the quality of the teachers, saying that some, having 'no Latin, no Greek or any of the classics', were unfit to prepare a clever boy for advanced education; whereas John MacKay of Hereford also blamed the system of *payment by results* — 'They work for results, for money results,' he said. This encouraged teachers to channel their energies into teaching the mass of the pupils, not just the bright ones, in preparation for the examination on H.M. Inspector's visit each year. To illustrate this — John Munro the teacher at Lionel presented 250 children for examination in 1882 and obtained a grant of £200. As number on the school roll was close on 300 and the average attendance 222, the grant would have been greater if he or the attendance officer had been able to persuade more children to come regularly. The *school boards,* local committees in each parish which built and ran the schools, were allowed to charge school-rates, which were expected to average out at less than 3d. in the pound in Scotland as a whole. But the expense of building the schools was so high in the Islands compared with the rents of crofts which were very low that in Barvas in Lewis in 1881 the school-rates were actually 6s.8d. in the pound! In 1883 they were still as high as 3s.8d., which made one old crofter in the parish complain, 'My bare rent is £3,7s., there is 10s.6d. for school rate and I have no child of school age!'

In thirty-three places still, mainly islands like Boreray (north of North Uist) and St Kilda, it was the Free Church Ladies Asociation which provided the school. In Boreray it was free: the children did not need to

The St Kilda children and the old people in 1886 with Mrs Ann MacKinlay, the nurse in the centre who had also taught the little ones and George Murray, the new teacher on the right.

pay fees, only to bring peats for the schoolmaster. Of the curriculum in these schools, John MacKay the minister said the children in St Kilda learned 'to read Gaelic and commit portions of Scripture to memory but nothing in the way of songs, nothing whatever — only the Psalms of David and the New Testament. They have no poets or poetry of their own.'

Ability and opportunity

Unwisely, being an incomer who had not been teaching long in Skye, Duncan Stewart expressed his opinion in public that Skye children were not so capable of learning as children in the south, and must be deficient in intellectual ability. He put the difference down to 'native habits' and only partly to not knowing English well. James Grant of Kilmuir took issue with him immediately:

'As one who knows the Highlands and Lowlands quite as well as the strange teacher in Stein (Duncan Stewart), I must differ from him in his opinion of the incapacity of Highland children. When they have competent teachers they learn as well as Lowland children, were their comforts at home the same, which I am sorry to say they are not.'

Alexander MacKenzie, author of *The Highland Clearances*, supported the minister, saying that he shared the view of William Jolly, H.M. Inspector of Schools in the Highlands, which was that with fewer advantages Highlanders progressed in education more than in the south.

Having to leave home to enter secondary education might be enough to prevent a clever child with poor parents from continuing at school; the nearest secondary school to Glenelg, for example, was in Inverness. But education added rungs to the ladder of opportunity for crofter children.

Two of the seven examination papers for Grammar School bursaries in 1883.

II.—BIBLE AND SHORTER CATECHISM.—Value 100.

One Hour allowed for this Paper.

1. Give a short account of Adonijah's conspiracy.

2. Where were the following placed in the temple :—The ark, the golden candlestick, the altar of incense, and the altar of burnt-offering ?

3. How was Solomon assisted in building the temple ? Why was David not permitted to build it ?

4. Where were the following places, and for what were they noted :—Eziongeber, Palmyra, Succoth, Upper Bethhoron, Joppa, and Thapsacus ?

5. What was Solomon's great sin, and how was he punished for it ?

6. What proofs did Solomon give of his great wisdom ?

7. Write out the answers in the Catechism which speak (1) of the Covenant of Life, (2) the Covenant of Grace, and (3) the change of the *day* of Rest.

8. Explain the following expressions :—Actual transgressions, want of conformity, no *mere* man, and *sensible* signs.

III.—ENGLISH.—Value 100.

One Hour allowed for this Paper.

I. GRAMMAR.

1. Write the plurals of—ship, gas, elf, cliff, brother, salmon, father-in-law, knight-templar ; the possessive singular and possessive plural of—man, book, goose ; the comparative degree of—good, fore, merry ; and the possessive plurals of—I, He, and It.

2. Write down the present indicative, past tense, and past participle of—blow, choose, burst, say ; write out fully the future indicate active and the future perfect indicative passive of any one of these verbs.

3. In the following passage parse the words in italics. How many statements are in it, and which, if any, are dependent ?

> " From *yonder* ivy-mantled tower
> The *moping owl* does to the moon complain
> Of *such as, wandering near* her secret bower,
> Molest *her* ancient solitary *reign*."

Derive *complain, ancient,* and *solitary.*

II. GEOGRAPHY.

1. Where are the following countries :—Spain, Persia, Italy, China, Egypt, Mexico, and Chili ? Name the capitals of all, and the chief rivers of any three of them.

2. Where are the following towns, and for what are they noted :—Quebec, Calcutta, Cork, Melbourne, Dunedin, Sheffield, and Bristol ?

III. HISTORY.

1. What happened at the following dates :—1174, 1263, 1297, 1314, 1513, and 1603 ?

2. What Scottish sovereigns were imprisoned in England for a lengthened period ? What led to their imprisonment, and by whom was Scotland ruled in their absence ?

If they persisted, they could become ministers, or come back as teachers who *could* speak Gaelic, or escape to jobs such as teaching in the cities and towns, and what they learned at school often gave them the ambition to break away.

By winning bursaries several of them gained the opportunity. An educational association for the parish of Rogart, for example, which John MacKay of Hereford helped to establish, already enabled boys to go to Aberdeen Grammar School and on to university to take degrees and become teachers. He said the association helped girls as well as boys, and also boys taking up trades e.g. as masons. Since 1869 the Free Church had been offering bursaries to boys aged about 18 leading on to grammar school and university, usually in Aberdeen, on a far wider scale. They gathered in many centres, some as far apart as Stornoway, Elgin, Rothesay and Tongue to sit seven papers including Latin, Greek and Mathematics in six and a half hours. The Latin papers lasted two hours and Gaelic half an hour, and some idea of the standard can be gained from two papers from the 1883 examination which are on page 119. A crofter's son from Gairloch scored the highest marks that year and four of the eleven bursaries went to boys from crofts.

First professor of Celtic in Edinburgh University, Donald MacKinnon from Colonsay, an example to every clever Highland boy.

Running the schools

A school board came into existence in every parish in 1872 to build and run the schools. Commonly it had seven members, elected by owners and occupiers of land worth £4 a year, a property qualification which denied a good many crofters the right to vote. The factor, the sheep farmers and the ministers were the most likely members, and factors tended to dominate the affairs of several school boards. Alexander MacDonald did in Skye where he was paid clerk and treasurer of the Portree and Snizort school boards and a member of five others. At Durness in Sutherland, Evander MacIver the factor expected to become chairman — 'I am appointed chairman in other parishes and none else will be mentioned here or it will be a slur upon the Duke of Sutherland.' In Lewis also William MacKay, the chamberlain of the Matheson estates, was chairman of all the school boards. Although the crofters paid more than half the school rates, the principle of 'no taxation without representation', which had lost Britain her American colonies, meant little to him. He said he could see no point in having a crofter on a school board.

'I always used my influence in advising them to send educated men,' he claimed, 'at least men who could sign their names. There are very few among the crofter class of sufficient intelligence to make useful members. I suppose the ordinary crofter here (Meavaig) would be of no great service on the board.'

Yet he had to admit that the parents of two of the teachers the school board employed in Uig were crofters!

The Report and What Came of It at Last

To complete its programme of meetings the Royal Commission arranged to listen to witnesses with Highland interests in Glasgow and Edinburgh. Then all the evidence they had heard which their shorthand writer had faithfully recorded was to be printed in full. That, in Fraser MacKintosh's eyes, would be the most important consequence of their mission. He said so publicly, soon after the Royal Commission's escape from drowning when the *Lively* went down, when he opened Inverness' new public library on 16th June:

'Whatever report the Commissioners may adopt, the mind of the country as to the condition, the usage and the requirements of these people (the crofters) will be made up, not from the report, but from the detailed evidence itself. Therefore the appearance of this evidence will be of the utmost importance and,' he added, relating his remarks to the occasion, 'the volumes, I hope, will find a place in every library in Scotland'.

Using the same argument publication of the other rich source — all the written information contained in the Returns the factors had made about the crofters, their land, their houses, their families and their animals — could have been equally justified. It was not published in full but appeared in an appendix only, in summary form for each estate. This was unfortunate, because it is a body of recorded information about the condition of Highland people, which is almost unique in Scottish history and which bears comparison with what William I's great Domesday Inquest had revealed about the people and the land in England in Norman times.

The Royal Commission and its staff established themselves in New Register House in Edinburgh where Lord Napier, Sheriff Nicolson and Professor MacKinnon were able to give its business a good deal of their time. Lord Napier took responsibility for the main question, the land, and the others each took on a section of the Report. All the Commissioners met for a solid week in January to discuss and revise their drafts, and over the following two months the committee of three, the chairman, the sheriff and the professor, acted as a revising group in finalising the Report. It was published along with all the evidence in five volumes on 28th April, less than a year since they had listened to the first of the crofters in Skye.

On the land question, the Report proposed to build on the idea of the *township*, where three or more crofters had some arable land and shared in the common pasture. The township would be a little community legally formed; it would be fenced and recorded, provided with roads half paid for by the landlord, and have access to all the peats, thatch, and sea-ware its members needed with no obligation to pay. Crofters in what a sheriff agreed was an 'overcrowded township' could compel the landlord to grant more land to the township to make their crofts bigger, if there was suitable land close by. If not, the landlord might, but need not, apply for grants from the Government to create new townships, to which any crofter who had been crowded out could opt to go. Fixity of tenure for all the crofters was not recommended, since it would not help crofters in the smallest crofts to make a living from the land alone: but fixity of tenure and compensation for improvements were to go to bigger crofters, paying rents of £6 or more, who undertook to put effort and money into the land on a 30-year lease.

This was a brave and original attempt by Lord Napier to solve a difficult problem but he failed to carry the Highland landlords on the Commission with him. They all signed the Report but three members added notes to explain their dissent on certain points. Fraser MacKintosh, wanting to benefit far more people, suggested lowering the qualifying rent to £4; Sir Kenneth MacKenzie, viewing common grazing rights as the greatest obstacle to improvement, favoured the creation of small farms, each with its own grazing instead; while Lochiel, in a memorandum nearly half the length of the section on land in the Report, preferred to see the landlord being the agent of change on his own estate, with help coming from the state in the form of loans.

The recommendations were a disappointment to many people. They disappointed the dreamers in the Highlands who in the words of the minister of Kilmuir imagined 'the Royal Commission and the Government can, as if with a magician's wand, make every crofter and cottar the happy possessor of horses, cattle, sheep and fish'. They disappointed those crofters who were hoping for 'the three F's', the Irish answer to the land question; and they disappointed the radicals in the flourishing Highland Land Law Reform Association who were demanding 'the land for the people'. Worst of all, they disappointed those witnesses who had been asked to specify in public the areas of land near their township which their people would like, because without a shadow of a doubt they and their neighbours had been encouraged to expect a lot more than the Commission could agree to deliver.

Nonetheless, by listening, probing sympathetically and allowing full expression to the crofters' grievances, Lord Napier's Commission served a most important function. By allowing crofters to 'let off steam', it acted as a safety valve but it was much more, since it channelled their grievances in the direction of Government and also brought them to the attention of people all over Britain through the newspapers. The way the crofters had given their evidence proved, incidentally, that they were as worthy of the right to vote as many who had it already; while the Commission's recommendations, impracticable though they might be, were sympathetic to the crofters' condition.

Without waiting to see what the Napier Report would recommend, the Highland Land Law Reform Association (the Land League) pressed ahead with the recruitment of members and the formation of branches in every part of the Highlands and Islands. In Skye John MacPherson, one of 'the Glendale martyrs', emerged as a persuasive advocate of land law reform and, inspired by stalwarts like him, branches of the League mushroomed all over Skye. Soon he was a full-time organiser for the League, travelling about the Highlands and speaking to huge, enthusiastic audiences who responded by establishing new branches. A thousand crofters came in to Oban, for example, to hear him and give backing to the campaign for votes for all crofters and reform of the land laws.

Four days later delegates from every branch from Barra to Orkney converged on Dingwall for the first national conference of the Land League. Predictably they rejected Lord Napier's proposals, demanding instead fixity of tenure for all at a fair rent assessed by a land court. They also wanted bigger crofts. To help to achieve these aims they further agreed that once they gained the right to vote they would use it only to

Memorial to the Glendale martyrs.

John MacPherson's house in his later life, still on the same croft at Lower Milovaig.

support candidates who were committed to land law reform. Within a year after the Dingwall conference the Land League had enrolled 15,000 national members, besides all the local members. There was so much sympathy for the League that in many places it was hard not to be a member, as the Kilmuir miller discovered when he saw the corn from his stacks blowing in the wind.

Having defined their aims the Land League now had the organisation to spread their message about the means — keeping up the pressure by non-payment of rent. The Kilmuir crofters, Norman Stewart of Valtos among them, refused to pay rent. At that time the price a crofter could get for any bullock he might have to sell fell so dramatically that very few could afford to pay anyway, and the rent strike spread. In some places, Grogary and Iochdar in South Uist and Uig and Glendale in Skye, crofters acting together seized neighbouring fields as pasture for their cattle with impunity, because a farmer and a shepherd or two did not dare to stop them. Nor could policemen or sheriff officers do their duty. When a party of nine policemen, including reinforcements from the mainland, set out on 30th October to go and maintain law and order in Kilmuir, they were stopped outside Uig by two hundred crofters armed with sticks, who went back with them, jostling them, tripping them and jeering at them for miles along the road to Portree. No heads were broken but the police had been humiliated: here was the proof that there was no law in Skye.

Determined to re-establish the rule of law, the Government agreed to the plan by the Chief Constable and the Sheriff to send in fifty extra police armed with revolvers, with a small fleet and over 400 Marines to protect them. This was the kind of action it had hoped to avoid when it established the Napier Commission in 1883.

The Marines landing in Uig Bay on 18th November met no resistance. Crofters with sticks knew they were no match for such a display of force and carried on working on their crofts instead, adopting a posture of passive resistance. Some Marines were stationed at Staffin, others at Hamara Lodge, Glendale, where a meeting of 600 Land League members closed quietly with prayers and melted away. The rent strike on the Kilmuir estate continued and spread through Lord MacDonald's and other estates in Skye. Thanks to the strength of the Marines on the one hand and the influence of John MacPherson over the crofters on the other, no confrontation ever took place and, having nothing to do, the

The Marines landing at Uig on Skye.

John MacPherson addressing a crowd of crofters in November 1884.

last of the Marines left Skye in the summer of 1885.

The crofters won by their illegal actions and using their new right to vote in 1885, when at a stroke they changed the face of Highland politics. Previously, landed families of whatever party had been able to treat the county constituencies as if they were their own, but now four out of the five Highland M.Ps., who included Fraser MacKintosh for Inverness-shire, were committed to land reform and they became known as 'the Crofters' Party'. Gladstone's Liberal Government, needing their support now for Irish Home Rule, was willing to act and using the Irish Land Act as a model, saw the Crofters Act through Parliament on 25th June 1886.

The Act applied to all the crofters irrespective of the amount of rent they paid and brought them practical benefits: security of tenure, the right to pass on the land to another member of the family, the right to compensation for improvements if they should ever give it up, and a new and permanent body, the Crofters' Commission, a land court with the power to fix fair rents. Controversy about the importance of the Act raged in June and July 1985 as soon as the Post Office, advised by the Historiographer Royal, Professor Gordon Donaldson, refused to issue a stamp to commemorate its centenary. He believed that the Act had ultimately been a disaster because it allowed many crofts to pass by inheritance to 'absentee tenants' who had no interest in them, but the weight of opinion among Scottish historians and crofting experts favoured the issue of a commemorative stamp. Dr T. M. Devine of Strathclyde University, for example, declared the Act to be a turning point in the lives of the Highland people. In a letter to *The Scotsman* on 5th July 1985 the former Secretary of the Crofters' Commission, Mr D. J. MacCuish, insisted that the 1886 Act required a crofter to be resident on his croft to benefit, and shrewdly assessed the Act as 'a remarkable breakthrough to special legislation for crofters in an age when proprietary rights were held sacrosanct.

It is true the Act did nothing for cottars who had no land, and nothing to transfer into the hands of crofters or cottars any of the land in the Highlands that was still feeding sheep and deer, but it did guarantee to Highland crofters that they could never be removed (a right envied by tenants in other parts of Britain) and that their rents would be fair, which meant lower in practice, about 25 per cent lower as a rule. The Act did not give the crofters the world but it made them secure in their own little patch, and that was no small gain.

Old houses made new beside Little Bay, Barra.

APPENDIX: Places of Meeting 1883

Skye

8 May, Tuesday	Braes:	Ollach Schoolhouse
9 May	Skeabost:	Snizort Free Church
10 May	Uig:	Schoolhouse
11 May	Stenscholl:	Schoolhouse
14 May, Monday	Stein, Waternish:	Schoolhouse
15 May	Dunvegan:	Church
16 May	Broadford:	Free Church
17 May	Isle Ornsay:	Schoolhouse
18 May	Bracadale:	Free Church
19 May	Glendale:	Free Church
21 May, Monday	Glendale:	Free Church
22 May	Raasay:	Torran Schoolhouse
23 May	Portree:	Court House
24 May	Portree:	Court House

Barra and the Uists

26 May, Saturday	Castlebay:	Schoolhouse
28 May, Monday	Lochboisdale:	Inn
29 May	Benbecula:	Torlum School Room
30 May	Locheport:	Free Church

Harris and Lewis

31 May	Obbe:	Schoolhouse
2 June, Saturday	St Kilda:	Free Church
4 June, Monday	Meavaig:	Free Church
5 June	Breasclete:	School
6 June	Barvas:	Free Church
7 June	Lionel:	Schoolhouse
8 June	Stornoway:	Drill Hall
9 June	Stornoway:	Drill Hall
11 June, Monday	Stornoway:	Drill Hall
12 June	Keose:	Church
13 June	Tarbert:	Free Church

Shetland

13 July, Friday	Lerwick:	Court House
14 July	Mid Yell:	Church

16 July, Monday	Baltasound:	Reading Room
17 July	Hillswick:	Northmavine Church
18 July	Foula:	'near the Schoolhouse'
19 July	Lerwick:	Court House

Orkney

20 July, Friday	Sanday:	Drill Hall a.m.
		U.P. Church p.m.
21 July	Harray:	Schoolhouse a.m.
	Birsay:	Schoolhouse p.m.
23 July, Monday	Kirkwall:	Court House

Sutherland

24 July	Bettyhill:	Farr Free Church
25 July	Bettyhill:	Farr Free Church
26 July	Kinlochbervie:	Free Church
27 July	Lochinver:	Church

Ross

30 July, Monday	Ullapool:	Free Church
31 July	Poolewe:	Church
1 August	Shieldaig:	Church
2 August	Balmacara:	Church
3 August	Glenshiel:	Church

Inverness

| 4 August | Glenelg: | Church |
| 6 August, Monday | Arisaig: | Church |

Argyll

7 August	Tiree:	Kirkapoll Church
8 August	Mull:	Bunessan Church
10 August	Tobermory:	Temperance Hall
11 August	Lochaline:	Church
13 August, Monday	Lismore:	Baptist Church

Caithness

| 4 October, Thursday | Lybster: | Free Church |

Sutherland

6 October	Helmsdale:	Free Church
8 October, Monday	Golspie:	Free Church
9 October	Bonar Bridge:	Drill Hall

Ross

| 10 October | Dingwall: | Free Church |

Inverness

11 October	Inverness:	Town Hall
12 October	Inverness:	Town Hall
13 October	Inverness:	Town Hall
15 October, Monday	Kingussie:	Court House
16 October	Kingussie:	Court House

In the South

19 October	Glasgow:	J.P. Court
20 October	Glasgow:	J.P. Court
22 October, Monday	Edinburgh:	Court of Justiciary
24 October	Edinburgh:	Court of Justiciary
26 December, Wednesday	Tarbert, Loch Fyne:	Public Hall

BIBLIOGRAPHY

I have intentionally based this book almost exclusively on two sources, the oral evidence the Napier Commission heard and its written records. Newspapers, *The Scotsman* and *The North British Daily Mail* chiefly, also helped to set the Commission's tour in time and place while *Fasti Ecclesiae Scoticanae* Vol 4 1923 and Vol 7 1928, and *Annals of the Free Church of Scotland 1843–1900*, 2 vols, provided information about the ministers who gave evidence.

Official Records (Scottish Record Office, Edinburgh)

A F 50   Royal Commission on the Crofters and Cottars in the Highlands and Islands of Scotland 1883–4.

A F 50   1. Minute Book

2. Entry Book of Out Letters

3. Register of In Letters 1883–4

4/1 to 4/1453   In letters 1883

5/1 to 5/159   In Letters 1884

7/1 to 7/19   Returns of crofters giving names, numbers of families and houses, rents, extent of arable and pasture, numbers of stock for the Highlands and Western Isles, not Orkney and Shetland.

8/1 to 8/7   Returns of cottars, giving names and occupations for the same area.

Official Publications

Report and Evidence of the Commissioners of Inquiry into the Conditions of the Crofters and Cottars in the Highlands and Islands of Scotland 1884   XXXII–XXXVI.

Return of Owners of Lands and Heritages, Scotland, 1874   LXXII

Report of the Royal Commission on Land for Deer Forests 1895, XXXVIII–XXXIX

Further Reading

A. Fenton, *The Northern Isles: Orkney and Shetland*, John Donald, 1978

A. Fenton, *Scottish Country Life*, John Donald, 1976

I. F. Grant, *Highland Folk Ways*, Routledge and Keegan Paul, 1961

M. Gray, *The Highland Economy 1750–1850*, Oliver and Boyd, 1957

I. F. Grigor, *Mightier than a Lord*, Acair, 1979

A. R. B. Haldane, *The Drove Roads of Scotland*, Nelson, 1952

J. Hunter, *The Making of the Crofting Community*, John Donald, 1976

J. Hunter, *The Politics of Land Reform 1873–95*, SHR L111, 1974

M. MacLeod, *Gaelic in Highland Education*, TGSI XL111, 1966

I. M. M. MacPhail, *Prelude to the Crofters' War*, TGSI XL1X, 1977

I. M. M. MacPhail, *The Napier Commission*, TGSI XLV111, 1976

I. M. M. MacPhail, *The Skye Military Expedition of 1884–5*, TGSI XLV111, 1976

W. Orr, *Deer Forests, Landlords and Crofters*, John Donald, 1982

E. Richards, *A History of the Highland Clearances*, Croom Helm, 1982

J. A. Smith, *The 1872 Education (Scotland) Act and Gaelic Education*, TGSI L1, 1980

Derek Thomson, *The Companion to Gaelic Scotland*, Blackwell 1984

W. P. L. Thomson, *The Little General and the Rousay Crofters*, John Donald, 1981

C. W. J. Withers, *Gaelic in Scotland 1698–1981*, John Donald, 1984

Index